By the same author

Skylarks and Seagulls
Buttercups and Brambles

Moorland and Meadow
Children of Portlethen

Elizabeth A Dodds

Published in 2020
with the help of Lumphanan Press
9 Anderson Terrace, Tarland,
Aberdeenshire, AB34 4YH

www.lumphananpress.co.uk

© Elizabeth A Dodds 2020

Printed and bound by Imprint Digital,
Upton Pyne, Devon, UK

ISBN: 978-1-5272-7515-7

Contents

Introduction — 7

Acknowledgements — 11

January: Darkness and Light — 15

February: Dressing-up — 29

March: Communion Sunday — 35

April: Dancing in the Rain — 43

May: The Circus — 51

June: Coronation Day — 67

July: An Orkney Wedding — 77

August: Follow My Leader — 99

September: Harvest Thanksgiving — 113

October: Holiday at Crieff Hydro — 121

November: The Flood — 149

December: Old Ways and New Beginnings — 159

Postscript — 169

For Kathleen, Sandy, Ralph, Morag, Marylen, Elsie, Hazel, Fran, Pat, Jacqui, and all our childhood friends.

Introduction

In 1939, my parents, Alexander Dunn and Florence Hourston, married and came to live in The Manse, Portlethen. My father had just been appointed minister of Portlethen Church and they arrived as newcomers, Dad from Beith in Ayrshire, Mum from Evie in the Orkney Islands, to make their home in a community where families had lived for generations, farming the land, or fishing in the seas offshore. The people of Portlethen extended a warm welcome to the new minister and his wife, and to us children when we arrived. We were all born at home in The Manse, Stuart in 1941, me in 1942, Marilyn in 1944 and Sandra in 1947.

When we were very young, the big stone house, its walled garden and courtyard were the extent of our world. We ate our meals round the scrubbed pine table in the kitchen, gathered in the evening in front of the peat fire in the drawing room. We ran along the paths in the garden, pushed each other on the swing that hung from the beech tree, kicked a football around the courtyard, played hide-and-seek in the old barns and stables.

As we grew older we spread our wings and ventured out beyond the boundaries of The Manse. We walked to Portlethen School on weekdays and to Church on Sundays. We fetched stamps from Miss Chalmer's Post Office for Dad and messages from Mrs Thompson's shop for Mum. We climbed trees and made dens in the Manse Wood, and played among the stooks in the fields at harvest time. We followed the tracks over Portlethen Moss in summer and sledged down the Post Office brae in winter. We stood on the railway bridge to watch the trains go by and paddled in the rock pools down at the shore.

From time to time, we journeyed beyond Portlethen and out into the wider world. We travelled into Aberdeen to go to music lessons on Friday night, to dancing lessons on Saturday morning. We went to the News Cinema in Diamond Street and to the Fair down at the Esplanade in summer. We picnicked among the sand dunes at Menie and drove to the Brig o' Feugh at Banchory to watch the salmon jump. We visited Aunt Mary and Uncle Danny at St Cyrus, and Aunt Nettie and Uncle Peter at Echt. Sometimes we were really adventurous and took the boat to Orkney to visit Granny Hourston and the aunts, uncles and cousins who lived there, or drove in the car all the way to Crieff for a holiday in The Hydro.

Like most people living in Portlethen at that time, we never ventured outside Scotland but the outside world regularly came to us. Every morning Dad read out stories from the *Press and Journal* about what was going on in the country and every evening the wireless was switched on for the 6 o'clock news. We grew up in the shadow of the Second World War and so we knew there were cities in Europe called Hamburg, Berlin, Paris and Amsterdam. In 1953 we listened to the news about the ascent of Mount Everest in Nepal, and followed preparations for the Coronation of Queen Elizabeth down in London. Our house was full of books and encyclopedias and atlases. I remember poring over the pages of the *"Wonders of the World"* and reading about the Pyramids in Egypt, Niagara Falls in Canada, the Great Wall of China, the Taj Mahal in India and the Parthenon in Athens.

Once a year, we caught a glimpse of life in faraway lands when the circus came to Aberdeen with its lions and chimpanzees from Africa, elephants and tigers from India, camels from Arabia, sea lions from the Arctic. Nowadays, training and display of wild animals is banned from circuses on ethical grounds but as children we never questioned it and loved watching the elephants lumber round the ring and the lions and tigers sit snarling on their pedestals in the cages.

Introduction

Unlike most of our childhood friends, we always knew that our home did not belong to us, that we lived in a "tied" house, courtesy of the Church of Scotland, and that some day our Dad would retire and we would have to leave The Manse, leave this community and set out into the world. I suspect our parents were, in their own way, preparing us for that day. By teaching and example, they were encouraging us to develop strong, independent characters, and giving us the skills and values that would help us to thrive in a world far away from our safe secure childhood home in Portlethen.

Elizabeth A Dodds (nee Dunn), 30th August 2020

Acknowledgements

These stories are a record of my own memories together with those of my brother and sisters and I want to thank Stuart Dunn, Marilyn Stronach and Sandra Edwards for their contributions. I am particularly grateful to Marilyn for her help in editing the text and for her suggestion to quote from the poem, "Scotland" by Alexander Gray. I also want to acknowledge a quotation from another poem, namely "A Poem for Winter" by Cecily E Pike.

I am grateful to Allan Dodds and John Edwards for their help in scanning old family photographs which have lain, yellowing with age, in boxes in our attics. When I first met Allan in Edinburgh in 1964, he was studying for a City and Guilds qualification in Photography at Napier College and he has used the skills he learned at that time to produce some of the images in this book including the oil lamp, the candles burning on the piano, and the standing stones in Orkney.

I want to acknowledge the skill of the unknown artist who painted the picture of a Scottish landscape that I have used on the cover of this book. I also want to thank Glen Ross of the Colours Gallery in Edinburgh for allowing me to use a detail of "Harvesting in East Lothian" by Robert Noble.

My very special thanks go to the young artist, Sean Robertson, a pupil at Portlethen Academy, for his beautiful drawing of my brother Stuart and I when we were pupils at Portlethen Primary School.

I would like to acknowledge the contribution of my cousins, Morag Sinclair, Marilyn Easton, and Lilian Hourston, along with my cousin Netta's friend, Agnes Work, in writing the story of my trip to Orkney in July 1953 to attend Netta's wedding. They provided lots of detailed information about what we saw and heard, who was there, what we ate and drank, particularly the Orkney tradition of "the bride's cog." I am also grateful to my mother, Florence Hourston, for the fund of stories she told us about her childhood in Orkney. I see a parallel between her vivid memories of life on the farm of Ploverhall in Evie and our clear memories of life in The Manse at Portlethen.

My thanks go to my playmate and school friend Kathleen Milne, now Mrs Kathleen Boyne from Stonehaven. She has offered her memories of how Portlethen celebrated Coronation Day and Harvest Thanksgiving which I have woven into the stories in this book.

I want to thank my friends here in Nottingham, particularly Jean, Susan, Margaret, Judith, Trish, Christine and Elvire, and my children, Jennifer and Jonathan, for their patience and support during the months and years when I have been telling them stories about a place in the north of Scotland, very remote from their lives here in the English Midlands.

I wish to acknowledge the invaluable contribution played by Duncan Lockerbie at The Lumphanan Press in helping me get this book and the two previous titles into print. I value enormously his constant calm, relaxed professionalism.

I am grateful for the encouragement given me by all the people who have read "Skylarks and Seagulls" and "Buttercups and Brambles," and have written and phoned and emailed to say how much they have enjoyed the stories. Some are members of the family who stayed with us at The Manse, while others are people who know my brother and sisters. Some have a connection with Portlethen, while others simply say the stories bring back memories of their childhood in different times and in other parts of the world. Because of them, I have written this third collection of stories about the lives of children growing up in a small farming community in North East Scotland in the years just after World War II.

January

Darkness and Light

It's Saturday night in The Manse at Portlethen and we're burrowed in behind the velvet curtains in the drawing room, noses pressed up against the glass of the bay window. The moon is shining but it's hard to see the outside world through the frost on the windowpane. I watch my sister, Marilyn, tracing the swirling patterns with her fingertip.

"It's a garden of ferns," she says.

"It's a nest of feathers," says little sister, Sandra. "Libby, what makes these pictures on the window?"

"Do you remember the poem in your reading book, Sandra?" I say.

"*Look out! Look out! Jack Frost is about! He's after your fingers and toes.*

And all through the night, the gay little sprite is working where nobody knows.

He'll climb each tree, so nimble is he, his silvery powder he'll shake.

Alexander Dunn, Florence Dunn, Sandra, Elizabeth, Stuart and Marilyn in the drawing room at The Manse, Portlethen

To windows he'll creep and while we're asleep, such wonderful pictures he'll make."

"If you look carefully, Sandra, you'll see Jack Frost painting feathery patterns on the windows."

"Where? Where is he? Libby, I can't see him," says Sandra, standing on her tiptoes, peering out into the darkness.

I breathe gently on the window and watch as the frost melts and disappears leaving an island of clear glass where I can see out into the garden. I watch snowflakes falling gently, floating down till they land on top of the garden wall, settling on the branches of the beech hedge, burying the lawn under a blanket of snow that sparkles in the silvery moonlight.

Behind me I hear the door open and Mum's voice scolding us,

"Bairns, bairns, where are you? Come away from that cold window at once. Come here to the fire. You need to get your hair dry before you go to bed."

It's Saturday night and at The Manse that means bath night when Mum washes our hair and makes sure we're scrubbed clean ready for church on Sunday morning. Now we're dressed in our pyjamas and snuggled into warm, woollen dressing gowns, ready for bed, but first we need to dry our hair. We lie down on our backs on the fireside rug, prop ourselves up on our elbows and tilt our heads towards the warmth of the peat fire. I look up towards the ceiling, watching as the beam from the electric light bulb dances through the swirling patterns in the lampshade. If I tip my head one way I can see my brother Stuart, trundling his cars and lorries along the rectangles and squares woven into the carpet, pretending he's following roads, stopping at crossroads, backing into parking spaces. If I tilt my head the other way I can see Granny, sitting still and quiet in the armchair, listening to the wireless.

I love my Granny Dunn. She is special because she's my godmother and I was named "Elizabeth" after her. When she was

Granny Dunn with her son, Alexander, in Beith, 1912

growing up, she was always called "Lizzy" and sometimes, when my Dad is talking to me, he calls me "Lizzy Anne." I wouldn't like anyone else calling me "Lizzy" but I don't mind when it's Dad.

Granny came to live with us when Stuart was a baby, before I was born, because she was slowly losing her sight, and wasn't able to manage on her own in her house in Beith in Ayrshire. When Granny first arrived, she could still see a little which was fortunate, particularly for Stuart. I have heard Mum tell the story of how she thought it would be healthy for Stuart and I as babies to have goat's milk to drink and so Dad bought a nanny goat and a young kid. At first the goats were able to roam around the grounds of The Manse but, unfortunately, one day the nanny goat ate Dad's best raincoat hanging on the washing line. Dad was not amused. After that, the goats were kept tethered to a post hammered into the ground on the grassy patch at the top of the courtyard. One day, when Stuart was three years old, he took hold of the rope that was tethering the baby goat and it ran round and round him, winding round his legs, round his body, round his neck until he was trussed up like a chicken and gradually being throttled. It was Granny Dunn who saw what was happening and raised the alarm, bringing Mum rushing to rescue her precious child. That was the last straw. The goats had to go!

Nowadays Granny Dunn is completely blind and can't see at all, but we take her hand and lead her wherever she wants to go. She's always gentle and kind, and never complains. I can't imagine what it must be like not being able to run around without worrying that I was going to bump into something, not being able to read my books or make jigsaws, not being able to ride my bike. I would complain very loudly all the time, but Granny sits quietly and patiently in her chair, sometimes staring into the distance, thinking her own thoughts, sometimes listening to the wireless as she is at the moment.

Moorland and Meadow: Children Of Portlethen

Granny Dunn, with Stuart in her arms, among the rose bushes in The Manse garden.

Grandpa Dunn at work as a furniture designer in Beith.

January: Darkness And Light

This evening I'm lying on the fireside rug at Granny's feet, shaking my head to help my hair dry more quickly. I can hear the crackle of the fire and, in the distance across the hallway, the creak of the pulley in the kitchen as Mum drapes the damp towels over the wooden bars, pulls on the ropes and sends the washing up to the ceiling to dry above the warmth from the stove. All around me are the familiar sights and sounds of a normal Saturday night in our house.

1950's wireless

Suddenly, everything changes! The electric light bulb hanging from the ceiling goes out, and we're plunged into darkness. The wireless shuts down and all is silence.

"What's happening?" asks Granny. "Why's the wireless not working?"

"I don't know, Granny," says Stuart. "The light's gone out. I think it's a power cut. I'll go and find out."

"I'm coming with you," I say.

"Me too. Me too," say Marilyn and Sandra, scrambling to their feet. No one wants to be left behind in the dark.

Out in the hall, it is pitch black. We shuffle our way along the wall, hands outstretched, feeling our way in the dark. Stuart reaches the

Moorland and Meadow: Children Of Portlethen

Candles burning on the Dunn family piano

kitchen door and pushes it open. We can't see anything but, out of the darkness, we hear rattling and rustling and then Dad's voice saying,

"Florrie, I can't find the torch. It should be here in this drawer."

"Alec, let me look," says Mum. "Is that you, bairns? Just stay where you are for a minute till we find the torch."

We hear Mum rummaging around in the drawer.

"Here it is," she says. We hear the click of a switch and see a faint beam of light shining out into the darkness, swinging over us as we stand in the doorway.

"Come in, come in," calls Dad. "We've got a power cut. Isn't this exciting? Now where do we keep the candles, Florrie?"

"They're in a box in the cupboard under the stairs," answers Mum who always knows where things are kept. I can tell Mum is frowning and, unlike Dad, finding it more annoying than exciting.

We follow the light from the torch till it disappears into the cupboard and wait anxiously till Dad reappears, blowing the dust and cobwebs off a box of long, white, waxy candles. Mum has found a box of matches in the kitchen drawer. She strikes one and holds the flame till it lights the wick on one of the candles.

"Stuart, can you take this candle through to the drawing room? Stick it in one of the brass candleholders on the piano. Make sure it's safe and then come back and I'll give you another one for the other side."

Off goes Stuart, out into the hall, cupping his hand round the flame to shield it from draughts. Mum lights another candle and holds it up so we can see. We pull up chairs at the kitchen table and sit down, watching in fascination as Dad uses a bread knife to cut one of the long candles into two, drips some hot wax onto a saucer and sticks the end of the short candle into the wax, holding it till it cools and sits firmly in place. He lights another and another and suddenly the kitchen is full of shining pools of light. I can see the faces of my little sisters glowing in the candlelight and the flickering flames dancing in their eyes.

"Right," says Dad. "So far, so good, but we need to light the oil-lamp as well. It's in the cupboard in the dining room, isn't it? See if you can find it, Florrie. I'll go and get some paraffin from the garage."

Dad takes the torch and off he goes outside into the frost and snow. Mum fetches the lamp and sets it on the kitchen table. She carefully lifts the glass chimney from its stand and wipes it gently with a cloth to get rid of any dust. We watch as she turns a knob and the thick cotton ribbon that forms the wick unrolls. Mum takes a pair of scissors out of the kitchen drawer and trims the wick, cutting off the burnt edges.

We hear the back door open and in comes Dad, stamping his feet on the mat, brushing the snow off his shoulders, setting down a can on the table. He unscrews the lid and the strong smell of paraffin drifts around the kitchen. He pours the pink liquid into the glass bowl of the lamp, lights a match and carries it to the wick till the flames dance and take hold. He sets the glass chimney back in place on the ring and winds the brass knob first one way, then another until the flame is adjusted and burns steadily. Suddenly the kitchen is full of light and we laugh and clap our hands in excitement.

"That's better," says Dad, smiling. I can see he's quite enjoying this adventure and so are we.

"Elizabeth," says Mum. "Can you take one of these candles and set it on the window ledge on the stairs? Marilyn, can you set this one on the hall table? Sandra, you come with me and we'll take this one to the bathroom."

Gradually we fill all the dark places in the house with pinpoints of light, chasing away the ghosts that lurk in hidden corners. Now we can see where we're going. We make our way back to the drawing room and push open the door. There's Stuart, kneeling on the fireside rug, poking the embers, setting the peat blazing. There's our

Granny, sitting in her armchair, leaning forward, chatting to Stuart, her face, usually so pale, glowing in the firelight. I can see two tall candles burning in brass candlesticks, lighting up the birds of paradise, carved out of different coloured wood, that flit across the front of the piano. Dad carries in the lamp and sets it on the shelf in the alcove next to the wireless. He turns and smiles at us.

"Now we've got light so we can see," he says, "and we've got the fire to keep us warm. The only thing we don't have is electricity to make the wireless work, so no music."

"What about the gramophone, Dad?" says Stuart. "That doesn't need electricity."

"What a good idea," says Dad.

Mum is frowning, looking a bit doubtful.

"Alec, it's nearly their bedtime," she says. "I'm just off to fill the hot water bottles and make their cocoa. I don't want them jumping around, getting all excited. There's to be no dance bands."

"Right," says Dad. "Stuart, will you wind up the gramophone and I'll look for some peaceful music."

Stuart starts winding the handle that sticks out of the side of the mahogany cabinet, turning and turning till it won't turn any more. Dad kneels down and opens the doors of the cupboard under the turntable where the records are kept and brings out some brown cardboard sleeves, reading the labels on the records, eventually choosing one. He slides it out of its sleeve, holding it carefully along the edge with his fingertips, dusting it with his handkerchief to remove any specks of dirt in the grooves. He stands up and gently sets the record down on the turntable. He opens the lid of the silver box with a picture of a dog and the words, "HIS MASTER'S VOICE," on the lid, and takes out a small steel needle, screwing it tightly into the holder on the arm of the gramophone. He switches on the clockwork motor and waits till the record is steadily circling round before very carefully lowering the needle onto the grooves. We hear the first swish coming through the fretwork grill at the front of the gramophone and then, into the cold dark winter night in a Scottish Manse, comes the warmth and sunshine of Italy as an orchestra plays and a man sings in a strange language from a faraway land.

"It's Caruso," says Dad. "He's a famous Italian tenor."

I listen carefully and, though I don't understand the words, I can tell he's singing of love and longing. I watch Granny, sitting quietly by the fireside, listening to the music. Is she ever lonely without her husband, dead and gone these fifteen years? Is she homesick for her friends and family still living in Beith? Is she sad because she is blind and can't see any more? She is surrounded by the love of her son and her grandchildren but still she has lost so much. Yet she never complains and always says "Thank you, dear" if one of us brings her a cup of tea, or takes her hand and leads her to her favourite rose bush in the garden so that she can bury her nose in the petals and breathe in the sweet scent.

After a while, the record ends and the music stops. Dad lifts the needle off the grooves and switches off the turntable. The door opens and in comes Mum, brisk and practical as ever, no time for sentimental Italians.

"Right, children, time for bed. Come to the kitchen and drink your cocoa. I've managed to heat some water on the stove for your hotwater bottles. Now brush your teeth. There's a candle in the bathroom so you can see."

All is hustle and bustle till we're ready to go upstairs. Mum has a candle on a saucer ready for each of us.

"Will you carry the candle, Libby?" whispers Marilyn. "I'm frightened it's going to topple over and burn me."

I climb the stairs slowly, carrying the candle, shielding the flame with my hand to keep it from blowing out. Marilyn carries the hot water bottles. I open the bedroom door, cross the room and set the candle down on the stone fireplace.

"Look," says Marilyn. She is standing at the window, pulling back the curtains and, suddenly, moonlight comes flooding into our bedroom, lighting up the darkness. We stand side by side, gazing out at the world through the swirling patterns of frost on the glass windowpane, and watch the light from the full moon shimmering on the snow lying on the rooftop of the barn, shining through the icicles hanging above the stable door, sparkling along the branches of the trees in the wood. We trace the line of the *Plough* tilting across the dark sky and search for the bright stars of *Orion's* belt, then turn away, leaving the curtains open to let the moonlight shine in. I blow gently on the candle till the flame flickers and dies. We snuggle down in our beds, say our prayers and drift off to sleep, while outside the moon and the stars light up the night sky.

February

Pupils from Portlethen Primary School, including Marilyn and Sandra Dunn, Wilma and Isobel Gray, Aileen Caird and Maureen Matthew, dressed up for a concert in the Jubilee Hall

Dressing-up

It's a cold, wet morning and Marilyn and I are standing at the attic window looking out over the waterlogged fields to the grey North Sea. We watch the rain sliding down the slate roof of the Manse, splashing into the gutter and gurgling down the drainpipe. We won't be able to go out to play in this weather.

We go downstairs to the kitchen. Mum is busy baking, creaming butter and sugar in a bowl to make shortbread. Our little sister, Sandra, is standing on a chair rolling out a piece of dough that's been left over from the scone mixture.

"Hello, darlings," says Mum. "Do you see that rain? You'll need to play inside this morning but remember your Aunt Lena's coming this afternoon and bringing two of her friends, so make sure you keep the house tidy."

We retreat back upstairs to the attic. We push open the door to Stuart's bedroom. He's sprawled on the floor making something with his Meccano and doesn't even look up. There's no point asking to play with him. If we're lucky he'll give us two or three bits of Meccano, perhaps a few nuts and screws, not even enough to make a wheelbarrow.

We go back out to the landing and look around, thinking of something to do. We see the door to the box room. We hardly ever go in there; everything is a jumble and smells old and damp and musty. Today, however, we turn the handle and pull open the door. There's a small skylight window, covered in dust and cobwebs but letting in enough daylight so that we can see a clutter of things piled high right up to the sloping ceiling. There are stacks of cardboard boxes full of books and papers, and piles of old black and white striped pillows with feathers sticking out of the seams. We can see an old bedside light with its shade scorched by the heat from a light bulb, and next to it, a wireless set with dials and buttons which don't work. I can see the brown leather suitcases that come out once a year when we go on holiday, and the box with the Christmas lights and decorations. There's the Santa Claus outfit which Mr Murray, the church elder, wears at the Sunday School Christmas party when he gives out presents to the children. I remember the year when we couldn't find the beard and Mum had to rush to make one with cotton wool glued onto paper. Mr Murray later complained that he nearly passed out with the fumes from the glue.

We burrow under a pile of blankets and old quilts and come across a large wooden chest. The lid is heavy and it takes both of us to heave it open and prop it against the wall. We peer inside. What a surprise! The chest is full of interesting things. One by one we lift them out and examine them. There's a green felt hat decorated with an ostrich feather, a cream silk jacket with tiny pearl buttons, and a crimson velvet evening gown with shiny black beading round the neckline. There are scratchy old tweed skirts and woollen jumpers smelling strongly of mothballs, but among them a shiny silver evening bag and a gold belt with a diamond buckle. There's a beautiful fur coat, lined with grey satin, and a white silk parasol painted with pink and red roses. At the bottom of the chest we find several pairs of soft leather shoes with tiny heels and delicate straps, and with them a mahogany box lined with purple velvet, full of jewellery, pearl necklaces, coloured beads, silver bracelets and enamelled hair combs. Hidden in a corner, we find a fox fur with beady glass eyes, pointed ears and a long bushy tail. It has four little legs dangling down and lever to open and close it's mouth.

Suddenly, I have a brainwave.

"I know what we'll do," I say. "We'll write a play and dress up in these clothes."

"Good idea," says Marilyn and off she goes to find a pencil and paper.

I ask Stuart if he'll take part and he agrees but only after I tell him he can build us a stage and organise the lighting. Sandra bounces up and down with excitement when I tell her she's to have a starring role in our play. She's only five years old but has an amazingly good memory. She can quote whole verses of the Bible off by heart after she's heard them in Sunday School.

All afternoon we prepare and practise and, in the evening after tea, we invite our audience of Mum and Dad, Aunt Lena and her two friends into the drawing room and show them to seats set out in a semicircle facing the stage which Stuart has made out of chairs draped with sheets and blankets, and lit by beams from several hidden torches. When everyone is ready, we switch off the main ceiling light and open the curtain of our theatre.

The play is a version of Little Red Riding Hood, with Sandra in the title role. She is wearing the silk jacket with the pearl buttons, and is draped in a red tablecloth fastened with a garnet brooch. She is carrying the parasol and the silver handbag, and has a basket of scones over her arm to take to her granny. I play her mother, dressed in the long crimson velvet gown with the green felt hat with the ostrich

Portlethen Primary School children dressed up for a production of the play "May Day in Welladay"

feather perched on my head. I'm festooned with bead necklaces and silver bracelets, and teetering on silver, high heeled, strappy shoes. Marilyn is the granny who's been eaten by the wolf and she's lying on a bed made up of chairs pushed together, dressed from head to toe in the fur coat with the fox fur hiding her fair curly hair. Stuart doesn't want to dress up so he wears his everyday clothes but shows he's the huntsman by swinging Dad's axe when he kills the wolf.

The play is a great success and everyone claps as we take our bow. Afterwards, while the visitors sit chatting and drinking cups of tea with Mum and Dad, we dismantle the stage, take off our dressing-up clothes and lay them carefully back in the chest in the attic. Sandra is hugging the fox fur, so lifelike with his bushy tail and bright eyes, and can't bear to think of him locked up in the dark. So later that evening our Little Red Riding Hood takes him upstairs to bed, lays her cheek against his soft fur and falls fast asleep.

March

Rev Alexander Dunn and the elders of Portlethen Church

Communion Sunday

Today is a special day for all of us in Portlethen Manse; today is Communion Sunday. Every Sunday is a bit special, but Communion Sunday is really special because, here in Portlethen, we celebrate Communion just twice a year, once in the Spring and once in the Autumn. All week Mum and Dad have been thinking and talking and preparing for today.

Last Sunday I heard Dad talking to some of the elders, asking them if they had managed to deliver all the Communion cards. In the weeks leading up to Communion Sunday the elders call at every house in the parish and leave cards for all the Church members. People then fill in the cards and hand them in at the door of the church when they come to the Service. This lets the minister and the Kirk Session know that they still want to be members and support the work of Portlethen Church.

On Monday, Dad brought a crate of red wine home from Aberdeen in the boot of his car. He carried the bottles into the house and stored them on the top shelf of the dining room cupboard alongside Mum's best Royal Doulton china dinner service. In the evening, when Mum was busy putting Sandra to bed upstairs, Marilyn and I tiptoed into the dining room and stood on a chair to sniff the cork stoppers on the bottles. What a strong smell, sort of fruity, and a bit musty! We're not used to having alcohol in the house because the Church of Scotland disapproves of people drinking beer or whisky or even wine, unless of course it's Communion wine.

Last Tuesday, Dad drove to the church and loaded up his car with boxes of linen that are kept in a cupboard in the vestry. He brought them home and dumped them on the kitchen table for Mum to inspect. On Wednesday, Mum washed all the cloths that were stained with red wine and then soaked them in Robin's starch and hung them on the line to dry.

On Thursday evening there was a big ironing session. Mum folded a blanket, covered it with a sheet, and draped it over half the kitchen table. She stood at one end wielding the electric iron and Marilyn and I sat on chairs at the other end ready to help. Sandra is too little to lend a hand, but she sat on a chair next to us and watched. Mum took a roll of linen out of the box and started unrolling, ironing, unrolling a bit more, ironing, sliding the linen along the table towards Marilyn and me so that we could reroll it. We worked together all evening, one roll after the other. It could have been boring but somehow it wasn't. The kitchen was cosy with warmth from the peat fire in the range and, for once, we had Mum's undivided attention. Usually she is so busy cooking and cleaning and keeping the house in order, always on the move, that it's difficult to get her to stop and listen, but now she had time to chat. So we talked about all sorts of things, about school and friends and where we would go on holiday, about Mum's childhood in Orkney, enjoying her company and knowing we were helping with something really important.

Last Friday after school we all went with Dad in the car when he took the boxes of linen back up to the church. Mum showed us how to dress the pews, unrolling the linen, draping the cloth over the shelf where we usually rest our hymnbooks, anchoring the cloth to the seat in front with silver clips. Dad and Maxie Gray, the beadle, set out an arc of chairs on the raised platform next to the pulpit for the elders to sit on during the service and spread a white linen tablecloth over the Communion table. Mr Gray brought silver salvers and cups from the vestry and set them out on the table ready for filling with bread and wine. After we'd finished, I stood at the door, waiting for Mum and Dad to do a last tour of inspection, and looked back at our church, at the sailing ship hanging from the ceiling, at the evening sunshine streaming in through the stain glass window, at the light reflecting off the snowy white linen and the silver cups. It seemed to me that our church had been transformed into a beautiful dining room, with its table set for a special meal, waiting patiently for the guests to arrive.

Preparations for Communion Sunday continued yesterday when Mitchell and Muill the baker's van drove into the courtyard just like it does every Saturday but this time Mum bought three extra white pan loaves. We watched her slicing each loaf, removing the crusts and cutting the bread into small squares. She placed them carefully on a linen cloth arranged over a silver tray, then folded the cloth over the bread to keep any specks of dust from falling on it. In the evening, Dad took the tray of bread and the bottles of wine in the boot of his car up to the church and left them in the vestry, satisfied that everything was now in place, ready for the Communion Service the next day.

Portlethen Church

So now it's Sunday morning and Mum and Dad are getting ready to go to church. Usually we go too but not today. Dad is wearing his dark suit and white dog collar, and is looking serious and thoughtful. He leaves early to go up to the church to change into his minister's gown and prepare himself for the service. Mum has on her best navy coat and high heeled shoes and is standing at the mirror in the hall adjusting her hat, the one with the feather in the brim. She takes her hatpin out of her mouth, brandishing it in her hand and talks to us sternly.

"Now, children," she says, "I want you all to behave yourself while we're gone. No playing out on the front lawn. You can play round the back but there's to be no shouting, and no kicking a ball. Stuart, do you hear me? And don't let the dog bark. You must all be quiet. Do you understand?"

"Yes, Mum," we chorus, following her to the door, watching as she walks briskly up the garden path and disappears out onto the Manse Road.

We close the front door and stand in the hall, a bit unsure what to do with ourselves. It's very seldom that Mum goes away from home and leaves us behind. We climb the stairs and stand at the front bedroom window watching as a procession of people walk up the Post Office brae, the ladies in their Sunday best coats and hats, the men in dark suits and ties. We see lots of cars drive by, bringing families in from the outlying farms around Cassieport and Cookston and Hillside. We're hoping for a last glimpse of Mum but the trees and bushes in the Manse Wood hide her from view.

We turn away from the window and think about what to do to pass the time. We can't skip or play ball in the courtyard because that could be noisy. We can't play hide and seek in the garden or have a swing because people could see us running around from the road. Stuart goes off to his bedroom to fetch his Meccano set and settles down on the path outside the back door with his flat plates, angle girders, wheels and axles. It's no use asking him if we can have some pieces to make something because he's always very reluctant to share. Marilyn and Sandra and I go out to the washhouse and fetch some of the little kittens that were born a few weeks ago. We sit on the doorstep and stroke their soft fur, listening to the gentle purrs. Sandra rocks one of the kittens in her arms and tucks it into her pram. Magnus, our dog, curls up at our feet. The house seems so quiet with everyone gone; even the hens in the barn seem to have gone to sleep. Time passes slowly as we wait.

Suddenly, in the distance, we hear the sound of cars starting up their engines, chugging down the road past the Jubilee Hall, past the Post Office, past Cookston Cottages. We know the Service is over and people are going home. We carry the kittens back to their pussycat mum in the washhouse and run to the back gate to watch for our Mum coming home. At last we see a car turn the corner, drive up the Manse Road and into the courtyard. It's not Dad's car; Dad is still up at the church with some of the elders, counting the collection on the table in the vestry, waiting while other members of the congregation help to remove the silver clips from the backs of the pews and roll up the linen cloths. Mum has come home with Mr and Mrs Sim, bringing Mrs Blacklaw and Mrs Milne to help wash up since there's no running water in the church. Together they unload the silver cups and bread baskets that were used by the elders at the Communion table, and carry in the wooden racks that hold the trays of small glasses, stained red with the dregs of wine drunk by the congregation. The kitchen fills with chatter and bustle and the strong, sweet smell of alcohol.

Mum gives Sandra a cuddle.

"Have you been a good girl?" she asks, smiling.

Sandra nods her head. We're all pleased that Mum's home again. We miss her when she goes away. Mum strokes Marilyn's curly head and says,

"Right, let's get to work."

Mum takes off her coat and hangs it on the coat stand in the hall, ties an apron round her waist and fills a basin of water at the sink with warm soapy water. Mrs Milne lifts one of the wooden trays from the rack and hands Marilyn two of the little glasses.

"Take these to your Mum. Hold them carefully," she says.

Mum washes all the glasses, the silver cups and salvers, trays and baskets while the other ladies dry them with dishtowels and set them back on the kitchen table. Stuart is busy wiping any spills of wine from the trays and polishing the wood till it shines. Then Marilyn and I set the little glasses carefully back in the felt lined grooves, eight to a wooden tray, and Stuart slots the trays back into the silver rack. While I work, I listen to the conversations going on around me and hear about the Communion Service, how the church was full, who was there and who wasn't, all the news about everyone in the parish. We wash, dry, put away, chat and laugh until the work is finished, then Mum takes off her apron and everyone sits down round the kitchen table and drinks a cup of tea.

We hear the sound of Magnus barking in the courtyard and open the back door to welcome Dad home. He is smiling, relaxed now that his work for the day is over and that everything went well. He tells us how pleased he was to see the church full of people and that they'd taken in a big collection to go towards Church of Scotland funds. Everyone agrees it has been a very successful Communion Service.

April

Elizabeth and Marilyn Dunn dressed in their kilts, ready to attend Eileen Ewen's Highland Dancing class.

Dancing in the Rain

It's Saturday morning and Marilyn and I are getting ready to go to Eileen Ewen's School of Dancing in Aberdeen. We're dressed in our kilts and white blouses and Mum is brushing Marilyn's curly hair, tying it back with a tartan ribbon.

"Look at that rain," she says. "Elizabeth, you'll need to wear your school coat with the hood. Have you got your dancing shoes in the bag? What about your swords? Have you packed them?"

We don't take real swords to dancing class. Our "swords" are just two wooden sticks screwed together so that they will pivot out into the shape of a cross. We need them for practising the *Sword Dance*.

"Can I go to dancing lessons?" asks my little sister Sandra. She's sharing the big chair by the fireplace with Magnus, our Shetland collie, cuddling him close, stroking his soft silky ears.

"Yes, darling, of course you can, when you're older," says Mum.

Dad has been quietly reading the *Press and Journal*, oblivious to the noise and chatter around him. Now he folds the paper, smiles at me and asks,

" Are we nearly ready to go? Is there any sign of Elsie?"

I see Mum frowning as she finishes tying the bow in Marilyn's hair, and hear her muttering,

"Poor Elsie! What a shame! She'll be soaking wet."

Just at that moment, we hear a knock on the back door and there's Elsie Main, sheltering under a very large umbrella, smiling cheerfully as Mum fusses around her. Every Saturday morning Elsie walks up to the Manse from her house in Old Portlethen, the fishing village down on the cliff top. Elsie's Dad is the skipper of the salmon cobble that goes out from Portlethen shore and he's one of the elders in the Church. Elsie comes to dancing classes with us and gets a lift into Aberdeen in our car.

Dad has taken his coat from its peg on the hallstand and is now outside, reversing the car out of the garage, honking the horn to tell us to hurry up. We grab the bag with our dancing shoes, pull the hood up on our school coats to keep our hair dry, say cheerio to everyone and run out to clamber into the car, Marilyn and me in the back seat, Elsie in the front next to Dad. Off we go. We splash through the puddles on the Manse Road, then it's up to the crossroads at Adam's Smiddy and out onto the Aberdeen Road. Dad is peering past the windscreen wipers as they swish to and fro, nursing the car along through a cloud of mud and spray thrown up by the buses and lorries, crawling past Hillside and the Check Bar, then rolling down the hill, over the Bridge of Dee and onto Holburn Street, turning left at Holburn Junction to park outside a big granite house in Albyn Place.

We all get out. Dad locks the car door, waves goodbye and sets off towards Holburn Junction. He spends his Saturday morning browsing around the Church of Scotland bookroom, chatting to the ladies who work there and choosing books and pictures and texts for the Sunday School. I'm not so keen on his latest acquisition, copies of "The Shorter Catechism." My Sunday School class is having to learn by heart all the answers to the questions, starting with number one, *"What is the chief end of man?"* and the answer, *"Man's chief end is to glorify God, and enjoy him forever,"* right through to question one hundred and seven. Anyway, I'll worry about that tomorrow; today I have to learn to dance.

Down the stairs to the school basement we go, into the cloakroom to hang our coats on pegs and change into our Highland dancing shoes. The cloakroom is full of noisy, chattering girls who all seem to know each other. I suspect lots of them go to the Aberdeen Girls High School or Albyn School for Girls or St Margaret's. We three country girls from Portlethen feel a bit like outsiders and so we keep our heads down and stick together.

When we're ready, we climb the wooden stairs to the ground floor hallway and make our way into a large room, filled with sunlight streaming in through tall windows. Miss Ewen is there, smiling to greet us, beautifully dressed as always, and so graceful in the way she moves. Mum says she started dancing as a young girl in the local area, originally as a Highland dancer, before going down south to the London School of Dance to continue her training in ballet and tap. Luckily, she then came back to settle in Aberdeen, open a school and teach lots of girls like us all the skills she'd learned.

Marilyn, Elsie and I find a seat on one of the low benches that run along the wall, tuck our swords and our bag of dancing shoes underneath and wait. When everyone is assembled, Miss Ewen claps her hands and all the girls form up in two lines, standing quietly, waiting for instructions. One Saturday morning, Mum came to watch us at our dancing class and was enormously impressed with Miss Ewen. Mum said that she wished she could clap her hands and we would all jump to attention.

Now we're ready for the Highland Dancing class to begin, starting

Moorland and Meadow: Children Of Portlethen

The Highland Fling

The Sword Dance

with the *Highland Fling*. Mrs Duncan on the piano sounds a chord, and we're off, Miss Ewen calling out the instructions.

"Hands on your hips, turn your feet out, point your toes, hands in the air, right foot first, then the left, listen to the music, round you go, and again, finish with a bow. Well done! Now, let's try that again. Change rows, back row come to the front. I want to see you up on your toes, light on your feet. Well done, girls! That's much better."

Miss Ewen gives us a short rest and then it's time to practise the *Siann Treubhas* and off we go again, following the music, gliding round in a circle, balancing on one leg, brushing the floor with the opposite foot, arms sweeping gracefully above our heads, then heels together, finishing with a bow from the waist.

Finally, it's time for the *Sword Dance* and we set our wooden crosses out on the floor and try very hard to jump nimbly from one quarter to the next without kicking the sticks and sending them flying. Every now and again there is a clatter and some poor girl is blushing with embarrassment as she retrieves her "swords" from wherever they've ended up. I think to myself it's just as well these are not real swords or quite a few of us would have lost a toe or two by now.

Finally, the Highland Dancing class is over and it's time for us to gather up our swords and change shoes for the ballet class. I don't much enjoy this class. I'm too anxious about not understanding the instructions because they're all in French and I don't know any French. I'll learn French when I get to Secondary School but at the moment I'm still in the Primary. Coming to ballet class means I've had to learn a few words; *plie* means bend your knees, *jete* means jump and *tendu* means point your toes, but mostly I just watch the older girls in the row in front and try to copy their steps. The trouble is that Miss Ewen keeps changing rows so that one minute you're in the back row, the next in the front. I breathe a sigh of relief when the ballet class is over.

It's time to change shoes again and, this time, it's on with our red shoes with their steel studs on the soles that we wear for tap dancing. I really enjoy this class. The music is bright and cheerful and at least the instructions are in English. We go *brush brush step* with one foot, *brush brush step* with the other, all the class tapping away together till the room echoes with the metallic sound and rhythm of a hundred hammering feet.

We're dancing to the music from the film *Singing in the Rain*, where Gene Kelly splashes along the pavement, twirling his umbrella. We're practising for the next show which, as usual, will be held in the Beach Pavilion down on the Esplanade. Eileen Ewen puts on a show every year and so we can look forward to lots of dance rehearsals, and fittings with Mrs McLachlan who organises the wardrobe department. Let's hope I don't have to dress as a frog this year! During the Interval last year, a few of us escaped the theatre and went for a paddle on the beach, still dressed as fairies and goblins, rabbits and rats. Mrs McLachlan was not amused when we returned with our costumes covered with wet sand.

Mum and Dad and Sandra look forward to coming to the shows and always say how much they enjoyed the performance and how well Marilyn and I danced. My brother Stuart has to be dragged along, protesting all the way.

Anyway, now the dancing lessons are over for the week. We grab our coats from the cloakroom and run out to find Dad sitting behind the wheel of the car, waiting patiently for us.

"Well, how did you get on?" he asks.

"Fine," I reply. "We're going to be dancing to *Singing in the Rain* at the next show."

"Are you?" says Dad, smiling.

Dad loves musicals and sings along with Fred Astaire or Judy Garland or Gene Kelly whenever their records are played on the wireless.

It's still raining as we drive home, the windscreen wipers on the little Singer struggling to cope with the downpour. We cross the bridge over the River Dee and catch a glimpse of the rushing current of water now threatening to overflow the banks. We chug slowly up the brae out of Aberdeen, following the main road towards Stonehaven. I hear Dad starting to sing softly,

"I'm singing in the rain, just singing in the rain,"

and we laugh and join in from the back seat,

"What a glorious feeling, I'm happy again."

We sing along until we reach the crossroads and turn left at Adam's Smiddy down towards Portlethen. Dad drives Elsie right to her door in Portlethen Village, and then we head for home and the warmth of the Manse kitchen where Mum and Stuart and Sandra are waiting to welcome us back. Marilyn and I tell them about the Show. Sandra claps her hands in excitement and asks, "Can I go?"

Stuart groans and asks, "Must I go?"

Marilyn and I ignore him, put on our dancing shoes, fetch umbrellas from the hallstand and tap around the kitchen floor, twirling our umbrellas and humming along to the chorus,

"I'm singing and dancing in the rain."

May

Parade of circus elephants through the city streets

The Circus

We're standing at the back bedroom window of The Manse, noses pressed up against the glass, peering out at the traffic as it whizzes by along the main road, watching out for something special. This morning, Chipperfields Circus is on its way north to Aberdeen and will be passing Portlethen. We know this because Dad told us, and he's standing at the window with us, just as excited as we are.

Dad loves circuses. Every Friday evening, after he's dropped us off at our music lessons in Aberdeen, he goes to the newsagents in Belmont Street and buys a copy of the *Worlds Fair*, a newspaper full of information about fairs and circuses, where they're playing, what new acts they're performing, how all the show people are getting along, their births, deaths and marriages.

"I can't see anything," says little sister Sandra, standing on tiptoe to peer over the window ledge.

"They'll be coming," says Dad, picking her up in his arms so that she can see over our heads. "You just need to be patient."

We stand quietly and wait, and I think about all the stories Dad has told us about how he came to be so interested in circuses. Nowadays, Dad is the minister of Portlethen but, when he was a student at Glasgow University, he spent his summer holidays travelling with the circuses, either Robert Brothers Circus or Pinder's Circus or Chipperfields. He drove their wagons, helped put up the Big Top, sold the tickets and the ice creams, fed the animals. He told us that once he had to be part of the group of acrobats and form a pyramid by standing on someone's shoulders. Another time he was the clown with the toothache, his face painted white and his mouth bright red. He wore a bandage wrapped round his head, and, when another clown hit him with a rubber hammer, out of his mouth popped an enormous tooth. We've seen the photograph that he keeps in the big black leather-bound Bible in the bookcase in the dining room. It's a picture of an elephant, standing with one foot raised, and alongside is a very pretty girl, dressed in a Hawaiian grass skirt and a garland of flowers in her hair, and, when you turn the photo over, someone has written, *"To Alec, with love from Rosie."* When we ask Dad,

"Is Rosie the girl or the elephant?" he just smiles, waggles his eyebrows and doesn't answer.

So here we all are standing beside Dad, looking out the bedroom window, waiting patiently for the arrival of the circus. I can see the hens scratching around the courtyard and some black and white cows grazing in the field below Balquharn. There's a blue Alexander's bus picking up passengers at the crossroads and a car turning into the driveway at Dr Horne's, but no sign of a circus.

"Look, I can see a truck," shouts my brother Stuart.

We crane our necks and sure enough, along the Stonehaven road, swinging round the bend past Portlethen Moss, rolls a big red truck dragging behind it a long wagon with the words *Chipperfields Circus* painted on the side.

"Well spotted, Stuart," says Dad. "That'll be carrying the tent poles and the canvas for the Big Top."

"I can see a truck pulling a caravan," squeals my sister Marilyn.

"That's where the circus people live while they're travelling," says Dad. "That's their home. You can see it's got four wheels and it's much bigger than an ordinary caravan. It has a kitchen and a living room and bedrooms and all the things we have in our house."

I wonder if there are children like us in the caravan? Are they looking out the window at our house? Are they playing with their toys or reading their books? Where do they go to school? Before I can ask Dad, around the bend and into view comes another long red truck, and then another. I peer at the writing on the side of the wagons, trying to make it out.

"It says, *Chipperfields Horses*," I read, "And *Chipperfields Tigers*."

We're so excited we can hardly stand still. How amazing to think there are lions and tigers prowling in their cages, rolling along the road past Portlethen, just a stone's throw away from our house.

"But where's the elephants?" wails Sandra. "I want to see the elephants."

"The elephants are too big to come in trucks, Sandra," explains Dad. "They'll be coming in the train this afternoon."

"Can we go and see the elephants?" pleads Sandra.

"Mmmm," says Dad, pretending he's just thinking about it, then he laughs to show he's teasing, and says,

"Of course we can."

So here we all are on the Esplanade at Aberdeen beach among crowds of people waiting for the arrival of the elephant parade. Dad has lifted Marilyn and Sandra up to sit on top of one of the concrete anti-tank blocks that line the pavement and is standing, leaning against the grey stone, with one arm round Sandra to make sure she doesn't fall off. Stuart and I stand in front of Dad, close to the edge of the pavement so we have a good view. The police have stopped the traffic so there are no cars driving past along the road. I listen for any sounds that the parade is on its way. I can hear a blast from a ship's funnel as it sails past the lighthouse and into the harbour and the call of a gull perched on the rooftop above the Beach Ballroom. I can hear a dog barking as it runs along the beach and the swish of the waves breaking against the sand and shingle.

At last in the distance comes the faint sound of a brass band, growing ever louder as it marches along the streets from the railway station to the Beach Boulevard, swinging into sight as it rounds the bend onto the Esplanade. Behind the musicians, we can see a man on stilts, looming over a gaggle of clowns who are cavorting along the street, darting into the crowds from time to time to shake hands with the little children. One of the clowns skips towards us, and then pauses, eyebrows raised, a big red-mouthed grin lighting up his white face as he stretches out an arm to grab Dad's hand and shake it enthusiastically.

"Hello, Alec," he beams. "What a surprise!"

"Hello, Tommy," says Dad. "Good to see you again. You're looking well."

"Coming to the show tomorrow?" asks the clown. " Of course you are. Call in and say hello to Mum. She'd love to see you. Sorry, can't stay and chat. See you."

Off he skips with a wave of his hand. Dad laughs and watches him go, completely oblivious to the stares from the people around us who are wondering how this ordinary looking gentleman in his brown tweed suit comes to know a clown in a circus. I'm not sure whether to feel pleased that we are special or embarrassed that we are attracting attention.

Anyhow, soon there is something much more interesting to see as along the street, padding softly on their big feet come the elephants, one behind the other, their long trunks snuffling along the tarmac, ears flapping. They are so close that we can see their wrinkled grey skin and their long eyelashes and the shiny toenails on their feet. We can hear the humph of their breathing as they plod by, and the rattle of the chains round their ankles and watch the thin straggly tails swishing from side to side as they disappear into the distance.

I turn and look at my little sisters, up on their perch. I can see Marilyn's eyes almost popping out of her head and Sandra laughing and clapping her hands in excitement.

"Did you enjoy that?" asks Dad, beaming at us.

"Yes, yes!" we answer. "Can we follow the elephants? Can we go and see where they live?"

"We won't be allowed into the menagerie – it doesn't open till after a performance," says Dad, "but we could go and see if Mrs Cowie is at home."

Dad lifts Marilyn and Sandra down from their perch, and holds their hands as we cross over the Esplanade to the other side. We run down the grassy slope on to the flat expanse of the links where usually we would see families walking their dogs or children flying kites or young lads kicking a ball about. Today it looks very different. I can see a tangle of striped canvas and ropes stretched out on the ground and hear the clink of metal as men, sleeves rolled up, swing their hammers, driving iron posts into the ground to anchor the guy-ropes of the Big Top. We follow Dad, picking our way through a maze of tents and trucks, with the smell of sawdust and hay and dung mingling with damp grass and diesel fumes. I can hear the clip clop of horses' hooves, the clink of harness, and the ominous growl of a lion as it pads to and fro behind the bars of its cage. I feel Marilyn clutch my hand.

"It's all right," I whisper. "The lions are locked up. They can't get out."

At last we reach a wagon with a set of white painted steps leading up to a red door. Dad climbs the steps, knocks and stands waiting. We hear a shuffling of footsteps, the door opens and there stands a plump, grey-haired lady.

"Alec Dunn," she beams, holding out her arms, "What a lovely surprise. Come in. Come in. Are these your children? Hello, hello. Tell me your names? Would you like a cup up tea, Alec? What about a glass of lemonade, Sandra? Sit down. Sit down."

So up the steps we go, into the wagon and sit down on a dark maroon leather settee. The circus lady bustles about handing everyone something to drink, then settles down in a chair for a chat with Dad. I listen for a while to their conversation, about which towns they'd visited, and how many people had turned out to see them and how everyone in the circus family was doing. I hear her telling him about some lady, a trapeze artist, who fell during the performance in Montrose and is now in the Aberdeen Royal Infirmary. I see Dad making a note of her name and the ward number and saying he'll go and visit her. Dad considers it to be one of his pastoral duties to act as chaplain to all the Circus and Fair people whenever they are in Aberdeen.

While Dad's catching up with all the circus news, I look around the wagon. It's as spick and span as a new pin, all glowing chestnut wood panelling and sparkly mirrors and soft red velvet cushions. On every shelf there is a display of wonderfully coloured glass vases and plates, crimson and turquoise blue and bottle green. I wonder how the lady manages to keep them safe when the wagon is travelling, bumping over pot-holed roads, swinging round tight bends. Do they ever get broken? Does she wrap them in tissue paper and pack them in cardboard boxes for the journey and then, as soon as the circus reaches a new site, does she carefully unwrap her glass vases and set them on the shelves? Does it make her feel at home when she can look around and see all her precious things? I would like to ask her but I'm too shy. So I sip my lemonade, say nothing

Interior of circus performer's wagon

until it is time to leave and we all say, "Thank you," and "Goodbye," and follow Dad down the steps and back to our car to go home.

Later in the afternoon, I wander around our house and notice things I've never really thought about before. Yes, there on the shelf in the drawing room is the white porcelain vase, painted with exotic birds of paradise, which Mum and Dad were given as a wedding present. On the mantelpiece above the fireplace is a daffodil yellow china jug with a gold handle and next to it a Royal Doulton figurine of a dancing lady in a long pink dress. Everywhere I look are precious things that Mum loves and is proud of in the same way as the circus lady. Thank goodness we don't have to take them down from the shelf every week and wrap them up to keep them safe when our house is on the move!

So now it's Saturday afternoon and we're off into Aberdeen to see the Circus. We queue up at the Box Office and buy our tickets along with everyone else but, when we reach the entrance to the Big Top, someone recognises Dad and shows us to special ringside seats, right at the front. The whole family is here. Mum, rather reluctantly, has come with us this time. Mum disapproves of circus people; she thinks they're like gypsies, always on the move, not part of normal society, a bit disreputable, not really suitable friends for a Church of Scotland minister and his family. However, I think she was worried that Dad on his own wouldn't look after us properly, that Stuart would be swinging on the trapeze, or Marilyn patting the chimpanzees or Sandra being eaten by the lions. So she's here, guarding her precious children, making sure we're all safe.

We're waiting for the Big Top to fill up with people and the performance to start. I pass the time by looking around me. I can see the main tent poles soaring skyward, supporting the swathes of canvas and festooned with ropes and ladders ready for the high wire acts. I can smell the sawdust in the ring, only a few feet away behind a low wooden barrier. I can hear the excited chatter from the audience and the toots from the brass band on their platform above the entrance as they tune their instruments.

Finally there is a fanfare of trumpets and through the curtains and into the circle of light comes the Ringmaster, resplendent in his red coat, black top hat and shiny red boots. He shouts out a hearty welcome and then is bundled unceremoniously out of the way by a group of clowns, waltzing into the ring in their big red lace-up shoes, knocking each other over, falling down, picking themselves up, pretending to hit each other, throwing custard pies. They get into a dilapidated car, start to drive around the ring until a cloud of smoke belches out of the engine and the wheels fall off. I laugh along with everyone else but really I find clowns a bit scary. I don't much like their white faces, their big red mouths stuck in a permanent grin, their wild shaggy wigs. I don't much enjoy slapstick humour, and feel guilty laughing when someone is hurt, even though it's only pretend. They sometimes pick on children in the audience and try to get them to come with them into the ring. We're in the front row. I just hope they don't come anywhere near us!

After a minute or two, the clowns stagger out. There is a pause, then the curtains are pulled back and into the ring gallops a string of beautiful palomino horses with gleaming golden coats and manes and tails the colour of buttermilk. Their bridles are studded with silver crystals, and plumes of pink ostrich feathers bob on their heads. They circle and glide in time to the music, weaving patterns round the trainer who is standing in the centre of the ring, directing their movements with the merest flick of the whip in his hand. Round and round they trot, sometimes in single file, sometimes in pairs, stopping from time to time to circle before flowing on once more, until with a graceful bow of their heads they turn and gallop out of the ring.

"Weren't they beautiful?" I whisper to Dad.

Other acts follow, one after the other. There are chimpanzees sitting at a table having a very messy tea party. There are sea lions clapping their flippers and dogs riding scooters and jumping through hoops. There are acrobats cart-wheeling and back-flipping and standing on each other's shoulders to form a pyramid. There are trapeze artists swooping above our heads, flying through the air to clutch at outstretched hands. We gasp and applaud and marvel at the bravery and skills of these circus performers.

At last, comes the moment Sandra has been waiting for. The band sounds a fanfare, the ringmaster shouts an introduction, the curtains are drawn back and into the ring marches the parade of elephants, each animal carrying a girl dressed in purple satin pantaloons on its back. Round and round the ring they plod, each elephant grasping the tail in front with its trunk. They're so close to us that we could almost reach out and touch them. Finally they come to a stop, raise a front foot to provide a step as their riders slip down from their backs and stand for a moment grasping a flapping ear and wave to the audience. Everyone applauds. Then the elephants gather round the trainer and follow his instructions. They stand on drums, barely big enough for four elephant size feet and circle round slowly, stepping as delicately as a ballerina. They sit on the drums, raising their front feet as if begging like a dog. They lie down in a row and pretend to be asleep. The climax of their show comes when the girls lie down on the ground in a row and one of the elephants steps carefully over their bodies. I wonder if this is why they are called "gentle giants" because everyone knows

Moorland and Meadow: Children Of Portlethen

that one careless step with a big foot would crush human bones. The audience goes wild and claps loudly in appreciation as the elephants leave the ring.

The next act is the tightrope walkers and we crane our necks upwards towards the roof of the Big Top as the performers inch slowly forwards balancing on the high wire. I'm clutching Dad's sleeve, dreading someone falling, when I hear a clink of metal coming from outside the tent.

Stuart pokes me in the arm and whispers,

"The lions are coming. They're building the tunnel."

I know they have to build a metal tunnel to bring the lions and tigers from their wagons into the ring. I hear gasps around me as a tightrope walker wobbles and almost falls but I am distracted, watching the construction of the cage being built in the centre of the ring.

The wirewalkers finish their act, climb down the ladder, take their bows and leave the ring. I can feel the sense of excitement rising as we wait for the circus workers to complete their preparations, rolling in pedestals of varying heights, setting them up along the edges of the cage. Finally, there is a roll of drums, a crash of a metal gate opening and into the ring rushes a string of lions and tigers leaping up to sit on the stools. I see Marilyn and Sandra shrink closer to Mum who wraps a protective arm round them, whispering words of reassurance.

The lion tamer enters the cage carrying only a short whip and a wooden chair. We watch spellbound as he encourages the animals to leap from platform to platform, to sit up and beg, to lie down at his command, to jump through hoops. Sometimes one animal will hop down from its stool and come towards him, snarling, lashing out with fierce-looking claws and bared teeth but the trainer faces it, armed only with the chair, and forces the lion back, back, back, a step at a time, up onto its stool. At the end of the performance the audience claps and cheers enthusiastically as the trainer opens the gate and one by one the animals hurtle through the tunnel and back to their wagons.

The circus is over. We leave the Big Top and skip back along the pavement to where the car is parked on The Esplanade.

"Did you enjoy that?" asks Dad, though he hardly needs to ask. "What did you like best?"

"The elephants," says Sandra. "They were enormous."

"I liked the chimps," says Marilyn. "They were funny."

"The lions and tigers" says Stuart. "Especially when they snarled."

"The horses," I say. "They were beautiful."

"But what about the clowns, the acrobats, the trapeze artists?" asks Dad.

I think about how to answer. Yes, the performers are clever, the trapeze artists are brave, and the clowns are funny, but what we really love about the circus are the animals.

June

Coronation of Queen Elizabeth in June 1953

Coronation Day

I wake up as the early morning light drifts in through the curtains and lie for a moment drowsily staring at the swirling patterns on the wallpaper above the fireplace. I have a feeling that today is a special day but for the moment can't remember why. I look over at Marilyn's curly head resting on the pillow in the bed opposite. She's still asleep.

My little sister's not very well just now and it makes me sad to think of her in pain and not able to play with us. Last week she had to leave home and go into hospital in Aberdeen for a hernia operation. When Mum and Dad went into the Royal Infirmary to visit her, they came home really upset because Marilyn had sobbed her heart out when they had to leave her behind in the ward. The next day, Mum had a word with the doctors, told them that she was a qualified nurse and, luckily, Marilyn was allowed to come home, even though she still had stitches in her tummy. We were very happy to see her, wanting to be kind and help her get better.

To begin with, she lay on the couch in the drawing room and we kept her company and read her stories. Later, when it was time to go out and play in the garden, Mum made a comfy bed of pillows and quilts in the old pram, and, even though Marilyn is eight years old and much too big for a baby's pram, Mum lifted her gently in, tucked the blankets round her, and Stuart, Sandra and I took turns of carefully wheeling her round the garden, letting her smell the sweet peas and roses, showing her how the strawberries were almost ripe. After a day or two, Dr Horne came and took the stitches out. She's able to walk around now but it still hurts and so she can't run and jump as usual, and she certainly can't dance.

Now, I remember why today is special. Today is Coronation Day! Princess Elizabeth is going to be crowned Queen Elizabeth in Westminster Abbey and in future we're going to have to sing, *"God save the Queen"* instead of the usual, *"God save the King."*

I think about the day I found out that things were going to change. I was sitting in the dining room at Mackie Academy along with my friends, Janet Hackett and Agnes Yeats, tucking into our school lunch, when I saw Mr Hutchinson, the Rector, come in and say something to the teachers and dining room staff. I saw the look of shock on their faces, and then heard the whispers rippling out from one group of children to the next till it reached our table.

"The King is dead," we heard. "The King is dead."

I saw some of the dinner ladies crying and wiping their eyes on their aprons. I knew something serious was happening, that perhaps I should be feeling upset, but I didn't really know the King. I'd seen his picture in the paper and heard him speak on the wireless but he was someone who lived in a palace in London, far away from us in Portlethen.

Anyway, that was more than a year ago and today is Coronation Day when the new Queen will be crowned in Westminster Abbey.

June: Coronation Day

All the children in the country have been given a day off school. Hurrah! I jump out of bed, get dressed and run downstairs. Mum and Dad are sitting at the kitchen table, drinking a cup of tea, and listening to the wireless. Mum looks up and smiles at me.

"Is Marilyn still asleep?" she asks.

"Yes," I answer, nodding my head.

"Good. Poor wee soul. The longer she sleeps the better."

Dad has his ear glued to the wireless.

"Do you know what has happened today?" he asks.

"Something to do with the Coronation?" I answer.

"Something else," he says. "We've climbed Mount Everest. The British have climbed Mount Everest."

This is exciting. I know that mountaineers from all different countries have been trying for years to reach the top of the highest mountain in the world. Now it sounds like we British have won the race. I feel proud of my country.

"So who was the first man to reach the top?" I ask,

"Well, there were two of them," answers Dad, "Edmund Hillary from New Zealand and Sherpa Tensing from Nepal. We don't know which of them actually took the first step onto the summit. They're not saying."

"But I thought you said that the British had climbed Everest?" I ask.

"Well, it was a British Expedition led by an Englishman, John Hunt," Dad explains.

"Hmm," not quite what I expected to hear but obviously Dad thinks it's something to celebrate. I pull up a chair at the table and Mum pours out my plate of porridge. We settle down to listen to the wireless and soon Sandra and Marilyn come and join us. Stuart is not interested and goes off somewhere on his bike. Dad goes out to fetch some peat for the fires and comes back shivering and stamping his feet.

Moorland and Meadow: Children Of Portlethen

Coronation procession in Westminster Abbey

Edmund Hillary and Tenzing Norgay on Mount Everest, 1953

"Goodness me, it's cold out there," says Dad, "More like November weather than June. I just hope it stays dry for this afternoon."

We can tell from the wireless that it's cold and wet in London. The reporter is interviewing people who have camped out on the pavement all night just so that they have a good view of the Coronation procession. He's commiserating with them about the awful weather but they all sound remarkably cheerful.

Soon, over the airwaves, we start to hear the clip clop of horses' hooves, the jingle of harness, the grinding wheels of the carriages as the procession makes its way through cheering crowds along the streets of London towards Westminster Abbey. The reporter tells us about the open top carriage with Queen Salote of Tonga, smiling and waving, completely oblivious to the cold and the rain. There's the Irish Stage Coach with the Queen Mother, wearing, we hear, a coronet set with the famous Koh-I-Noor diamond. Finally comes the team of dappled grey horses pulling the Gold State Coach carrying the Queen and the Duke of Edinburgh.

We listen as the man from the BBC describes the scene in Westminster Abbey. I know that television cameras are broadcasting to homes around the country but no one we know in Portlethen has a television set and so we listen to the words on the wireless and turn them into pictures in our mind. We see the royal blue carpet forming a path from the church door down the centre of the nave, the scarlet uniforms of the heralds, the ermine capes of the dukes and earls, the diamond studded tiaras of the peeresses, the long white tunics of the sultans and sheiks from the Arab states, the golden orb and sceptre lying on a crimson velvet cushion. We listen to the names of all the famous people in the procession, the Duke of Gloucester, the Duke of Kent, Earl Mountbatten, Viscount Montgomery of Alamein, the Duke of Wellington, Prime Minister Winston Churchill, the Prime Ministers of all the Commonwealth countries, the Moderator of the Church of Scotland, the Archbishop of Canterbury. We hear the music from the orchestra soaring up to the vaulted ceiling of the great cathedral, and a fanfare from the buglers echoing among the pillars and carved stone screens. We see the young Queen in her beautifully embroidered dress take her place on the throne, and know she is sitting above the Stone of Destiny, brought from Scone Palace, and used in the coronations of all the Kings and Queens of Scotland. We listen to the solemn vows she makes to serve her people and hear the words ring out from the congregation, "God save the Queen."

Now it's the turn of Portlethen to celebrate the Coronation. We're holding a Gala in the field up at the crossroads right next to Adam's Smiddy but, after the pomp and pageantry and colour of London, this is a bit of a disappointment. The sky is grey and overcast with dark rain clouds and not a blink of sunshine or a glimpse of blue sky anywhere. Parked in the centre of the field, criss-crossed with ruts and muddy tyre tracks, are three or four lorries, decorated with strings of bunting flapping in the cold North Sea wind. There are a few trestle tables with ladies from the WRI, the Women's Rural Institute, handing out cakes and lemonade to a scatter of local people, well wrapped up in tweed coats and woollen hats.

I'm standing shivering on the back of a float under a banner that reads "Portlethen Parish Church and Sunday School." Elsie Main and I are just about to dance the *Highland Fling* as our contribution to the general entertainment. Marilyn should have been dancing as well but she's still recovering from her operation and so there's just the two of us, poised to demonstrate what we've learned at Eileen Ewen's School of Dancing in Aberdeen. I'm feeling really self-conscious, well aware I'm not the world's best Highland dancer, regretting not feeling able to say "No" when Dad asked me. So here I stand in my short-sleeved white blouse, tartan kilt, black laced dancing shoes, my long red hair tied back with a tartan ribbon.

Elsie and I take up our position, toes turned out, shoulders straight, hands on hips, ready to start when Dad drops the needle onto the record on the portable gramophone.

As I wait, I glance at the little crowd of people gathered in front of the float. There's Mrs Main and some of her friends and family from Portlethen Village, here to support Elsie. There's Mum, smiling encouragingly, holding my coat over her arm, sheltering Sandra and Marilyn from the gusty wind. I smile at Marilyn, wishing she were up here beside me. Goodness me! I've just spotted Stuart sidling up to stand at the back of the crowd. Well that's a surprise! I wasn't expecting any support from my dear brother. He protests loudly when he's dragged along to end of term concerts at our dancing school. I wonder if Mum has had a word with him?

We wait nervously, Elsie and I. Dad seems to be having a bit of a problem with the gramophone. I can hear music coming from the Portlethen School float over to my left and can just make out my friends, Kathleen and Sandy Milne, among a group of children dressed in Tyrolean costume, skipping around in a dance that seems to involve a lot of thigh slapping. They look like they're enjoying their performance.

At last, I hear the first chord of the music from Jimmy Shand's dance band, glance across at Elsie and together we bow from the waist. Then we're up on our toes, first one hand raised, then the other, circling round, point the right foot, tap your calf with the left foot, heel-toe, remembering the steps. We hop from one foot to the other, till it's the last twirl and we take a final bow. There's polite applause from the audience, a "Well done, girls," from Dad and it's over. Thank goodness! I jump down from the lorry.

"Well done, Elizabeth," says Mum. "You danced beautifully. Goodness me, child, you're frozen. Now get your coat on before you catch your death of cold."

Mum shepherds us along the edge of the field to where Dad's car

Moorland and Meadow: Children Of Portlethen

Portlethen Primary School children in the field next to Adam's Smiddy with the radar pylons in the background. The group includes Sandra Dunn, Jacqui Wright, Isobel Gray, Wilma Gray, Maureen Rothnie, Hazel Mitchell, Kathleen Wood, Marilyn Dunn and Bertha Arthur

Coronation mug, 1953

is parked and bundles us inside, fussing over Marilyn, saying she should be lying down in a warm bed.

"Stuart, go and tell your father he'll need to come and drive us home. These children are frozen and I need to get them somewhere warm."

"But what about our free gift?" protests Sandra from the back seat. "I'm not going till I've got my free gift."

"Ach," says Mum, with that funny sound she makes when she's exasperated. "Stuart, go and tell your father to drive us home and then ask Mr Kingdom over there if we can have our free gifts now because we're going home early."

Off gallops Stuart and is back in a minute clutching four pale blue enamel mugs with a picture of the Queen painted on the side. He hands one to each of us. Inside the mug is a cellophane packet full of round pink and orange and lemon Oddfellows. I untie the purple ribbon from around the top of the packet and suddenly the car is filled with the warm, spicy smell of cinnamon. I pop a sweet into my mouth. Delicious! And another. And another. Some taste of lemon, some of strawberry but the very best orangey-brown ones taste of cinnamon.

Just then Dad appears, jangling his car keys, smiling, saying,

"These look good. Is there one for me?"

We drive back home to the Manse and run inside to huddle round the range in the kitchen to warm our hands and feet.

At bedtime, we sit round the kitchen table in our dressing gowns and Mum gives us each a cup of cocoa in our Coronation mugs. Later, as I lie in bed, I think about the day. If I'm honest, I can't say that this Coronation Day was wonderfully exciting and enjoyable, but it was different and a bit special. I suspect it is a day I will remember.

July

The wedding of Netta Wood and Fred Sinclair in Evie, Orkney

An Orkney Wedding

The evening sun is setting over the Island of Rousay as we swing left off the main Evie road and drive up the bumpy farm track towards Ploverhall. Aunt Mary turns around, smiling at me and Marylen, slumped wearily in the back seat of the car.

"We're almost there, girls," she says.

"Thank goodness," I think to myself, but I'm too polite to say it out loud. It has been such a long journey.

It all started when the invitation arrived in the post from Aunt Annie and Uncle Alec for our family in Portlethen to go to the wedding of their daughter, Netta, up in Orkney. I heard Mum and Dad talking, saying they would love to go, but with children and hens and Church commitments it was impossible. Then came a phone call from Aunt Mary and Uncle Danny in St Cyrus saying that they were going to Netta's wedding and would Elizabeth like to go with them as company for their daughter, Marylen. I was so excited! I felt special. I would be the only one from our family going to the

Moorland and Meadow: Children Of Portlethen

Stuart, Elizabeth, Marilyn and Sandra Dunn with cousin Marylen Hourston and Magnus, the dog

Stuart, Elizabeth, Florence and Sandra Dunn on St Cyrus beach with Aunt Mary, and cousins Ian, Billy, Lily and Marylen Hourston and Edith Howie

wedding, off on an adventure, without my brother and sisters. I would be travelling with my cousin, Marylen. I like Marylen. She often comes to stay with us at The Manse. She joins in all our games and is really good fun.

So I packed my small brown leather suitcase, waved "Goodbye" to everyone in Portlethen, jumped into the back of Uncle Danny's car and off we went, driving through Aberdeenshire, past fields, across rivers, through villages and towns till we reached the farm of *Brae* near Keith where Mum's brother, Sandy, lives and that's where we spent the night.

This morning we were up at dawn, driving north, past Inverness, past Dornoch, past Brora, past Helmsdale, dropping down to Berriedale, crossing bridges and burns and moorland, climbing up hillsides, swinging round bends, the road getting narrower and twistier the further we went.

"Are you alright in the back?" asked Aunt Mary, noticing that I was very quiet.

"I think I'm going to be sick. Can I get out?" I whispered.

Uncle Danny screeched to a stop and out I scrambled, standing shivering miserably on the roadside. Aunt Mary put her arm round me, whispering words of comfort but I could see Uncle Danny was looking at his watch, anxious about reaching the north coast in time to catch the ferry to Orkney. So I climbed back into the car, closed my eyes, willing the journey to be over.

At long last, we reached Scrabster and there was the St Ola tied up alongside the pier, puffing steam and smoke from its funnel. We made our way up the gangway as the ship's crane lifted Uncle Danny's car, swung it round and lowered it down into the hold. The dockers on the pier untied the hawsers and off we sailed out of the harbour into the wild waters of the Pentland Firth. Marylen and I climbed to the top deck, leaning over the railings to watch the windswept moorland on Dunnet Head glide by.

Florence Dunn in the uniform of a district nurse
out rowing with Mary Hutchinson

Once out into the tides and currents of the Pentland Firth, the boat caught the swell and began plunging up and down, rolling from side to side, lurching upright. Aunt Mary, looking miserably pale and queasy, joined us on deck.

"I hate this crossing," she said. "I'm always seasick. I'm going to find a bench and lie down." Off she staggered, with Marylen following closely behind.

Somehow, I felt fine. I'd been so carsick on the drive north that it was a relief to get out in the fresh air. I planted my feet firmly on the deck, grasped the handrail and kept my eyes fixed on the prow of the boat, trying to stay upright. Soon we reached the southern tip of the island of Hoy and followed the line of red sandstone cliffs northwards. I watched the gulls wheeling above the shoreline and could just make out the rows of guillemots and kittiwakes perched precariously on rocky ledges. On we sailed, ploughing through the waves till we reached the massive stone stack that they call "The Old Man of Hoy" and then it was round the corner into calmer waters, gliding past the island of Graemsay. As we sailed past the lighthouse on the island, I thought about Mum's friend, Mary Hutchinson, who comes to stay with us in Portlethen every summer. She lives in Stromness but teaches in the school on the island of Graemsay. Every weekday morning, come rain or shine, she sails her boat over to the island and then sails back to the mainland in the evening when her day's work is done. How interesting! I don't know anyone in Portlethen who goes to school every day by boat.

Soon the ship was slowing to manoeuvre gently alongside the pier at Stromness. Marylen and Aunt Mary, looking a lot happier now that the sea crossing was behind them, came and joined me. As we waited for Uncle Danny's car to be offloaded, I scanned the boats tied up along the shore, wondering which was the one that carried the schoolteacher over to Graemsay everyday.

Then it was back into the car, bumping along the narrow cobbled streets of Stromness, out onto the open road following the signposts to Finstown. We drove through farmland with fields of oats and potatoes and grazing cattle, but not a tree in sight because it's too windy in Orkney for trees to grow. We drove past the standing stones at Stenness, much bigger than the stone circle on top of the hill overlooking Portlethen. We passed a grassy mound in the middle of a field that Aunt Mary said was called "Maeshow". She told us that it's a Stone Age burial tomb and that we know that the Vikings visited it a thousand years ago because they left writing on the walls saying, *"Haakon took the treasure out of this mound."*

I was in the middle of wondering where Haakon took the treasure and what became of it when I noticed a signpost pointing left towards Dounby and I remembered all the stories Mum has told us.

"Uncle Danny, did you go to Dounby Market when you were little?" I asked.

"I certainly did," said Uncle Danny. "Has your Mum been talking to you?"

Moorland and Meadow: Children Of Portlethen

The Hourston family farm of Ploverhall in Evie, Orkney

The Hourston Family, including Nettie, Davy, Alec, Danny, Edith, Bill, Mary, Jimmy, Annie, Eva, Granny, Lily, Winnie, Ivy, Grandpa and Florence

"Yes," I replied. "She loved going to Dounby Market. She said it was the best day in the year, that you used to offer to do odd jobs for your neighbours, perhaps weeding their gardens or carrying baskets of peat or digging up potatoes, anything to earn a penny or two to spend at Dounby Market."

"That's right," said Uncle Danny. "Did she tell you how every year Father would pretend that we wouldn't be going that year, that he was too busy, that the horse was lame and how we used to beg and plead until he laughed, saying he was only teasing? We'd be awake early in the morning, hardly able to sit still and eat our breakfast because we were so excited. Father would harness the old horse, Rose, to the cart and we'd all jump in, wave goodbye to Mother and off we'd go, clip clopping along the road, up over the hill and down the other side till we reached Dounby."

"What was it like, Uncle Danny?" I asked.

"Well, Father would go off and talk to the other farmers and look at the animals, the big Clydesdale horses, the cattle, the pigs. Sandy and Davie and I, we liked the fairground rides. There were lots of stalls selling fruit and cakes and sweets and every year the girls would buy something special to take home to Mother- an orange, a melon, a coconut. One year Nettie tried to bring an ice cream back but it melted and disappeared long before we got back home."

As Uncle Danny was talking, we arrived at Finstown and swung northwest, following the coast, with the islands of Gairsay and Wyre and Rousay out to sea, until we came to Evie. We passed the church and turned off the main road, heading inland up a farm track.

So here we are, almost at journey's end. I can see the light shining out from the windows of Ploverhall and the door opening. There's Mum's brother, Davie, alongside Aunt Peg and cousin Wilfred, on the doorstep waiting to welcome us. There's hugs and handshakes and cries of, "Come awa' in," and through the door we go into the warm, welcoming kitchen of Ploverhall.

"My lass, how you've grown," says Aunt Peg. "Sit ye doon. You must be hungry. Now what would you like to drink?"

There's a scraping of chairs on the stone floor and soon we're all sitting round the table enjoying a feast of ham and potatoes, of crumbly oatcakes and slices cut from a round of Orkney cheese. There are scones with butter and bramble jelly, and plates of sponge cakes and shortbread, all served with cups of tea poured out of a big brown shiny teapot. I listen to the voices of the Orcadians, so warm and lilting, just like Mum's back home, and I think of all the stories Mum has told me about her childhood here in this house.

I can see the box bed along one wall of the kitchen where Granny and Grandpa Hourston slept and where Mum and all her brothers and sisters were born. I can see the basket of peats beside the black iron range where the food was cooked. I remember Mum saying,

"We were brought up on herrings and brose," and how her mother used to say,

"Eat that or you won't get anything else and if you eat that you won't need anything else."

Mum told us that her father and brothers always got served first when they came in from working in the fields, and that the girls had to wait till they were finished before they could sit down and eat. Mum has kept up the tradition because, when we sit down for a meal back home in Portlethen, Mum serves Dad first, then Stuart and afterwards us girls. Perhaps I should protest but somehow we're used to it.

My eye wanders to the space on the wall next to the door where Mum told us her father hung his fiddle. On dark winter nights, he would get it down from its hook and play for his children. Her brothers would push back the table and they would all dance while their mother sat knitting in her armchair, rocking the baby's cradle with her foot.

I'm hearing the music, seeing the cradle rocking, until in the warmth of the kitchen I'm not sure if I'm awake or asleep and dreaming. Aunt Peg notices and says,

"You girls need to be in your beds. Come with me and I'll show you where you're sleeping."

Marylen and I follow her up the narrow wooden stairs to the attic bedroom and we tumble into bed and are off to sleep in no time.

I wake up next morning with the light of dawn creeping in through the skylight window and lie for a moment listening to the slow breathing from my cousin in the bed next to me. I think to myself that this is the room where my Mum slept all these years ago. I remember her telling me how the attic in Ploverhall was divided into two by a partition with the boys sleeping in one half, the girls in the other. Mum shared a bed with her sister, Eva, and every morning it was their job to wake their little sisters, the twins Lily and Ivy, and get them dressed, ready for school. Mum told me that Eva had beautiful long wavy auburn hair and used to stand every morning brushing and brushing it till it shone. Mum's sisters Edith, Nettie, Eva, Lily and Ivy all have curly auburn hair like their father. Mum felt really jealous because she had straight dark hair, like her mother. I can just imagine her standing here in this attic room, quickly combing her hair and tying it into plaits, scowling at Eva slowly brushing her hair till it glowed like fire.

After a few minutes, Marylen wakes up and we lie for a minute chatting and giggling over nothing much. We get up, get dressed, go downstairs and eat our breakfast of porridge and creamy milk straight from the cow. The wedding isn't till this evening so there's plenty of time. Uncle Davie and Wilfred are out tending the animals, with Uncle Danny helping out. Aunt Peg is sharing family news with

Aunt Mary, chatting over a cup of tea, and so Marylen and I put on our jackets and go out to explore. We follow the farm track up between the fields, up onto the moorland and rough grass on Burgar Hill, up till we reach the banks where generations of Hourstons have dug peats for their fires. We sit down on a clump of heather to catch our breath.

I look back down the hill towards the sea, over the fields of Ploverhall, Hourston land that has been farmed by my grandfather, and his father and grandfather before him. I can see the other stone-built farms of Evie, hugging the hillside, sheltering from the wind, and I can hear my Mum's voice chanting their Norse names, Georth, Grugar, Creyan, Gruna, Feolquoy, Nidgarth. I can see Spithersquoy where my cousin, Netta, lives. I wonder how she's feeling this morning as she wakes on this her wedding day.

Beyond the fields of Spithersquoy, just offshore, lies the little island of Eynhallow. I remember Mum telling me that as a child she longed to visit Eynhallow. She pleaded with her father to take her out in his boat when he went fishing but he always said the waters around Eynhallow were too dangerous to go anywhere near. She pestered her brothers to take her until one day Danny and Davie relented and said she could come with them when they went fishing. They rowed up onto the little beach on Eynhallow, told her she had to be quick because the tide was coming in. Mum said she jumped out of the boat, ran round and round in a circle on the beach and then hopped back in the boat, absolutely delighted with herself. Now every time she looked across at Eynhallow she could say, "I've been there."

From my perch on the hillside, I can see the road that Mum walked along everyday on her way to the school at Costa. It's a bright sunny summer's day today but Mum has told me about the struggle the little children faced walking home from school on a dark cold winter's evening with a gale force wind blowing and the rain lashing down. On days when the weather was particularly bad, her mother used to send her son, Davie, to meet his younger brothers and sisters. Mum told me that Davie would open the buttons on his long tweed coat, clasp the lapels in his hands and stretch his coat out to form a windbreak. All the little children would huddle in behind him, sheltered from the storm, until they reached the warmth and safety of home.

I lie back on the rough grass, listening to the sound of the lapwings and curlews up on Burgar Hill, breathing in the scent of peat and heather, and I think of all the stories Mum tells us about this moorland.

The cows at Ploverhall were milked in the morning and then taken up to the hill to roam and graze on the rough pasture during the day. It seems to have been Davie's job to take the cows up the road in the morning, because Mum says that every time she hears a woodpigeon cooing from the rooftops round The Manse in Portlethen she thinks she hears her mother's voice calling,

"Tak twa coos, Davie. Tak twa coos."

Every day, after school it was the job of all of the young ones to go up the hill and find the cows and bring them home for the evening milking. Mum tells us that sometimes the cows had wandered off and they would be out on the hill searching and calling on dark winter evenings, knowing they couldn't go home until they found the beasts. At other times, on warm summer evenings, when the cows were close by and easily gathered in, there was time to play.

"Let's go and find Lowrie's Water," I say to Marylen, scrambling to my feet, eager to be off exploring, following in the footsteps of all the Hourston children in times past.

We skip along the track through the heather until we find a small loch, with dark peat-brown water and shallows bright with marsh marigolds and yellow flag iris. This was the playground for the children of Ploverhall. Mum tells us of the fun she had with her brothers

Moorland and Meadow: Children Of Portlethen

Lowries Water, Evie, Orkney

Grandpa Hourston at his peat stack on Burgar Hill in Orkney

and sisters, paddling in the shallow water on hot summer days, leaping from one grassy island to the next, sailing their boats made from partan shells. Marylen and I trace our way round the edge of the loch, jumping over water channels, stepping gingerly through patches of damp sphagnum moss, trying to keep our shoes and socks dry, until we reach the main path and head back down the farm track to Ploverhall.

After lunch, while the uncles and aunts are chatting over their cup of tea, Marylen and I wander through to the sitting room, used only for special occasions. Marylen fetches a box with dress dolls that she's brought with her in her suitcase. We lay them out on the window ledge, along with their paper wardrobe of clothes for all occasions.

"Let's pretend that they're going to a wedding," suggests Marylen and so we try on this dress, that coat, a matching hat and handbag, wrapping the paper tags round the cardboard dolls to keep the clothes in place, chatting as we make up imaginary conversations. As we play, I remember something Mum told me about this window ledge. When she was a little girl, she had a friend at school who was sent for piano lessons. Mum desperately wanted to be able to play the piano but her parents couldn't afford to pay for lessons. So she drew a piano on the window ledge in Ploverhall, marking out the black and white keys, and sat for hours running her fingers over the pretend notes, singing to herself.

In the afternoon, Uncle Danny says we're all going to take a walk down the hill to visit Granny Hourston and Winnie at Bayview. There's no Grandpa Hourston now: he died before I was born. As he got older, he decided it was time to hand farming at Ploverhall over to his son, Davie, and move with his wife and daughter, Winnie, to Bayview, not far away. So off we go, Uncle Danny, Aunt Mary,

Moorland and Meadow: Children Of Portlethen

Aunt Annie, Aunt Ivy, Florence Dunn, cousins Netta Wood, Morag, Evelyn, Tom and Jean Sinclair, and Elizabeth Dunn with Granny Hourston in Evie, Orkney

Cousins Jean, Morag, Tom and Evelyn Sinclair with Stuart and Elizabeth Dunn in Finstown, Orkney

Marylen and I, marching down the farm track, skipping over the puddles, out along the main road till we reach the big white house called Bayview. We make our way up the garden path, past a tangle of weeds and old rose bushes and knock on the door. It opens and there's Granny Hourston, taller than I had expected, grey hair in a bun, wearing a long black woollen skirt.

"Come awa' in," she says, leading us into the kitchen with its scrubbed wooden table and warm peat-burning fire. On either side of the fire are two comfy armchairs, one for Granny, one for Winnie. Winnie is one of Mum's little sisters and she has Down's syndrome. She never went to school and has always lived at home, loved and protected by all the family. Uncle Danny gives her a big hug and crouches down to talk to her. She has her own language and is a bit hard to understand but she shows us her mouth organ and plays us a melancholy little tune. Marylen and I sit for a while on the hard kitchen chairs, listening to the adults talking, and then ask if we can go and explore.

We climb the stairs, peeking into empty bedrooms, opening empty wardrobes, creaking open cupboard doors to find empty shelves. I can't help thinking how different it would have been if Granny and Grandpa had been living here when they still had fourteen young ones at home. There would have been children in every bedroom, the sound of footsteps clattering down the stairs, shouts and laughter filling the hallways. Now the house feels rather forlorn, full of shadows.

We make our way back downstairs to the kitchen just in time to hear Uncle Danny asking,

"Are you going to the wedding, Mother?"

"No, we're staying home," says Granny Hourston, "but Netta's going to come in by and show us her dress and the flowers and perhaps bring a bit of the wedding cake."

We say our goodbyes and walk back along the road towards

Moorland and Meadow: Children Of Portlethen

Aunt Lily, Mary Hutchinson, cousins Florence,
Billy and Evelyn Moar at The Manse, Portlethen

Cousin Netta Wood and Agnes Stevenson
in the courtyard at The Manse

Ploverhall. Aunt Mary and Uncle Danny and Marylen are chatting quite happily but somehow I'm thinking about all the things I've just seen and feeling a bit sad. I can still hear Winnie's plaintive little tune echoing in my ears and see all those empty rooms. I decide that, when I think of Granny Hourston in Orkney, I'm not going to remember her in Bayview. I'm going to picture her sitting in her armchair in Ploverhall, rocking the cradle with one foot, clapping her hands and laughing as she watches her husband playing his fiddle and all her children dancing around her.

It's early evening and we're sitting in the Evie Church waiting for the wedding to start. I'm wondering if this is the same church where Grandpa Hourston used to pass sweeties to his children on a Sunday morning to encourage them to sit still during the long sermons. I look around the congregation and spot lots of his offspring, now grown-up with families of their own. There's his daughter, Lily, with her husband, Willie Moar, and my six Moar cousins from Birsay. There's Ivy and her husband, Ernest Sinclair from Finstown, sitting next to cousin Morag, and the little twins, Tom and Jean. Their sister, Evelyn, isn't there because she's the flower girl and will be coming to church later with the bride. There's Aunt Eva, her beautiful auburn hair that Mum envied so much tucked neatly under her hat. She's sitting next to her husband, Gordon, and son, Robson. And there's Aunt Annie sitting in the front row, waiting anxiously for the arrival of her husband and very special daughter, Netta, the bride.

  I notice a group of older girls sitting together to one side. They must all be friends of Netta because I recognize one of them, Agnes Stevenson. She's not a relative but used to come and stay with us at The Manse, sometimes with Netta, sometimes on her own when she started training as a nurse at Aberdeen Royal Infirmary. Right at the front I can see the dark curly hair of Fred Sinclair, the bridegroom, and his best man, Eddie Seatter, standing with their backs to the congregation, fidgeting nervously as they wait.

At last we hear the organ start to play The Bridal March, and down the aisle comes Netta, walking slowly on the arm of her father. Netta is dressed in a beautiful white satin gown, with a fine lace veil covering her dark auburn hair. Behind Netta walks the bridesmaid, my cousin Edith, wearing a long, pale blue dress and a band of flowers in her fair hair. I know Edith quite well because she came up from Ayrshire with her mum to stay with us at The Manse in Portlethen during the War to be safe from the bombing nearby in Glasgow. Walking behind the bridesmaid is the flower girl, my cousin Evelyn, looking very pretty, carrying a posy of pink roses.

We stand to sing hymns, listen to a prayer and a short talk from the minister. Fred and Netta make their vows, they sign the register and the wedding is over. Netta and Fred, now Mr. and Mrs. Sinclair, walk slowly down the aisle, smiling at all the people who have come to wish them well, and we follow them out into the light of a warm summer evening in Orkney. Immediately, there's a squealing and a wailing as two sets of bagpipes are blown into life and there's Uncle Earnest, Morag's Dad, and Willie Sinclair, the bridegroom's brother, dressed in their kilts and sporrans and black velvet jackets, ready to pipe us along the road to the Reception. We form a procession and off we go, following the pipers and the bride and groom, walking along the main road through Evie till we come to the Drill Hall.

Inside, we hang up our coats, sit down at long tables and tuck into a hearty meal of homegrown Orkney food. Everyone drinks a toast to *"The Happy Couple"* and listens to speeches from the bridegroom and a very nervous Best Man. After the meal, the tables are pushed back against the wall and the floor cleared ready for the dancing. Out come the tins of *Slipperine* and I watch as the powder is sprinkled over the floor to make it slippery enough for the dancing. Meantime the band of local Evie musicians has been setting up their instruments on the stage, and now they're busy tuning up their fiddles, playing a few chords on the piano accordions, beating the drums, ready to play.

The dance starts with the *Grand March*, with the bride and groom leading the procession round the dance floor, followed by the bridesmaid and best man, the mother and father of the bride, and then everyone joining in. Afterwards it's one dance after another, all the familiar ones I know from school and Church socials. I dance the *Gay Gordons* with Morag. Uncle Danny takes Marylen and I up for *The Dashing White Sergeant*. I dance with my Birsay cousins, with folk I know and folk I don't know. We clap and yell in the *Eightsome Reel* and swing till we're dizzy in *Strip the Willow*. I can feel the floorboards beneath my feet dance along with us, bouncing up and down to the rhythm of the music.

There's a pause in the dancing, and I go and sit down beside Aunt Mary and sip lemonade from a glass. I watch as a big wooden bowl full of some steaming hot liquid is passed along from one guest to the next.

"What are they drinking?" I ask Aunt Mary.

"That's the *bride's cog*," she answers. "It's a mixture of home brewed ale and whisky, a dash of sugar and a few spices. It's a bit of a mystery what exactly is in it because every family has a traditional recipe for the *bride's cog* which they keep secret."

I notice that they don't offer the cog to the children, which is just as well because it doesn't look very hygienic to me, everyone drinking out of the same bowl. It doesn't seem to bother anyone else because they're swigging away and laughing heartily, looking like they're really enjoying themselves.

"What time is it?" I ask Aunt Mary.

"It's after midnight, darling. Are you tired?"

I shake my head. Amazing! I'm usually sound asleep in bed by this time but somehow tonight I'm wide-awake.

Standing stones at the Loch of Stenness in Orkney

Marylen nudges me and points. I realize that not everyone in the hall is awake. Along the front of the stage is a row of little Moses baskets with babies and toddlers, tucked up under warm blankets, sound asleep amid all the shouting and clapping and stamping feet.

At one o'clock in the morning, out come the tables again and supper is served. There are sandwiches and bannocks, cakes and shortbread, all served with lots of cups of tea for the grownups. There are oranges and sweets and lemonade for the children and I fill up my plate and munch away. I can't believe I'm eating like this in the middle of the night! Wait till I tell everyone back home!

About three o'clock in the morning it's all over. We join hands and sing *Auld Lang Syne*. We fetch our coats from the cloakroom, say goodbye to everyone, join Aunt Peg and Uncle Davie to walk back along the road to Ploverhall. The moon is setting and the sky glows with the golden light of dawn just breaking over Eynhallow Sound. We pass Bayview and I can picture Granny Hourston and Winnie snuggled up in their beds. I wonder if Netta and Fred managed to slip away from the reception for a minute or two so that they could show Granny Hourston and Winnie the wedding dress and the flowers and perhaps take them a piece of cake? Now that all the excitement is over, I feel tired and trudge wearily up the farm track, climb the stairs to our bed in the attic of Ploverhall and fall asleep to the distant sound of waves breaking along the Evie shore and dreamy memories of an Orkney wedding.

August

Stuart and Elizabeth Dunn. Drawing by Sean Robertson, former pupil of Portlethen Academy

Follow My Leader

It's a fine summer evening and we're playing up in Portlethen Moss. We know this place like the back of our hands and run along the tracks through the heather, jumping over the ditches, skirting round the deep dark pools and tiptoeing our way through the soggy sphagnum moss that carpets the low-lying areas where peat was dug out in days gone by. My brother, Stuart, leads the way as usual because he's the oldest. I'm following close behind, with our little sister, Marilyn, trotting at my heels. Bringing up the rear are the twins, Kathleen and Sandy Milne, our friends from up the Manse Road in Gushetneuk.

We weren't really expecting to be up in the Moss this evening. It was Stuart's idea. We'd just finished a game of rounders in the courtyard back home at The Manse when Sandy said,

"What will we play at now?"

"Let's go up to the Moss," said Stuart.

So here we all are, running through the heather, following our

Moorland and Meadow: Children Of Portlethen

Stuart Dunn and friends, Stuart Thompson, Ralph Horne and Derek Crichton in the courtyard of The Manse, Portlethen

The family from Gushetneuk including Mr Milne, Kathleen and Sandy Milne with Elizabeth and Marilyn Dunn

leader, off on an expedition. We're not really dressed for being up in the Moss; we usually have on our old dungarees to protect our legs from being scratched by woody twigs, and wellington boots to keep our feet dry. So we have to be a bit careful and watch where we're going. We skip by the Milne's bank, inspecting the rows of peat slabs lying among the heather like cold, dead soldiers, waiting for some miracle that will see them spring into life in a blaze of light and warmth. We leave them to their slumbers and run on again, following the path, balancing along wooden planks over deep ditches, skirting round clumps of birch and alder, heading for our peat bank, the one belonging to the minister of Portlethen Church, where our Dad is digging this year.

I'm following Stuart because that is what I'm used to doing. Stuart is just fifteen months older than me. I followed my brother very closely into this world and I've been following him ever since. I've followed him up trees, over dykes and ditches, up and down the cliffs at the shore. I've followed him to school, always in the class below, known to teachers as Stuart Dunn's sister, copying him, learning from him how to ride a bike, how to mend a puncture, how to find birds' nests, how to climb over the rafters above the garage. Most of the time, my habit of following Stuart has taken me to interesting places and lots of good fun but sometimes it has led me into terrible scrapes.

Anyway here I am, following Stuart, for better or for worse, trotting along at his heels, off on an expedition. We reach our peat bank and stand for a moment looking around. We can see where Dad has started setting up our peats to help them dry, leaning four slabs against each other like the poles of a wigwam, then balancing one peat across the top as a roof to keep the rain off. We'll be up in the Moss again this weekend with Dad to finish setting up the peat and there they'll sit all summer until September when the tractor and cart will come and we'll bring them home to the Manse. Marilyn,

Moorland and Meadow: Children Of Portlethen

Stuart and Elizabeth Dunn

always the most conscientious among us, bends down and starts setting up one or two more little houses.

"Come on, Marilyn, we'll do that another time," I say, and make my way round the back of the bank to my favourite place, a little mound covered in a carpet of heather so deep that you can disappear in it. I lie down on my back and Marilyn and Kathleen join me, nestling into our bed amongst the woody stalks, knowing no one can see us. We rest quietly, looking up at the sky, watching the clouds drift by, listening to the gentle hum of the bees and the distant trill of a skylark high above us. I breathe in the sweet scent of gorse, stretch out my arms, running my fingers gently over the clusters of heather blossom, and think to myself,

"This is a magic place. I could stay here forever."

Suddenly I hear a shout and a thump and the peace is broken. I sit up and look around. There's Stuart and Sandy lining up at the top of the bank then leaping off, flying down onto the soft boggy area where Dad has just been digging. I look at Kathleen and Marilyn lying contentedly among the heather, then scramble to my feet, making my way to join my brother, following his lead as always.

I stand at the top of the bank and hesitate. It looks a long way down but I know Stuart will call me a *feartie* if I back out now. So I grit my teeth, take a short run and jump, down, down until my feet squelch into the soft wet peat. Whew! Survived! I scramble up and turn to watch as Kathleen follows me down. Then it's Marilyn's turn. She's two years younger than me but sometimes I forget that because she's as brave as a lion and determined to keep up with me. I wait at the bottom of the bank, wanting to shout encouragement but knowing she doesn't like a fuss. She runs, jumps and down she flies, sinking deep into the spongiest, most waterlogged patch, her feet disappearing till she's buried up to her knees. I see her struggling to pull her feet out of the bog and grab hold of her round the waist, tugging her legs free with a squelch and a plop.

Moorland and Meadow: Children Of Portlethen

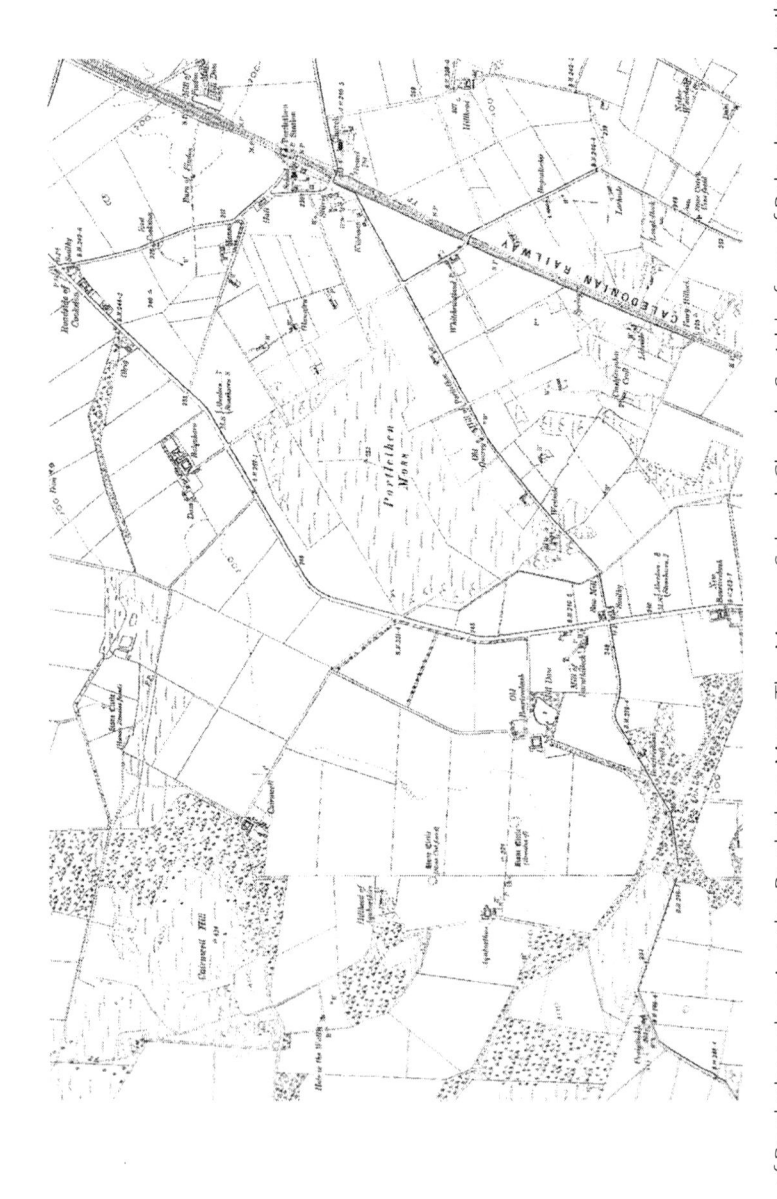

Map of Portlethen showing the Portlethen Moss, The Manse, School, Church, Smiddy, farm of Balquharn and railway line

"I've lost my shoe," she cries, hopping on one foot.

"Hold onto me," I say, kneeling down, plunging my arm into the hole and pulling out one very wet, soggy shoe. Marilyn pushes her foot into it, staring at it in dismay.

"Look at my socks. Look at my shoes. They're all brown and wet. Mum will give me a row," she whispers, her lip wobbling, eyes full of tears. Marilyn hardly ever gets a row from Mum, not like me. She always tries to be good and do what she's told and is broken-hearted if Mum so much as frowns at her.

Stuart and I look at each other. We hate seeing Marilyn looking worried and upset. Our little sister is often quiet and shy with strangers, but with us she's always chatty and smiley. I notice Stuart frowning and know he's thinking, searching for a solution, wondering how to make Marilyn happy again.

"What we need, Marilyn, is a fire to dry your socks," he announces.

"But how are we going to light a fire?" I ask. "We haven't any matches."

"Yes, we have," answers Stuart.

Well, that's a surprise! Puzzled, I watch him turn and disappear round the back of the bank, wondering what he's up to. The only time I ever see matches up in the Moss is when Dad produces a box from his pocket and sets fire to a patch of heather on top of the bank to burn it off. This makes it easier for him to slice through the turf when he's preparing to open up a new bit of bank.

After a minute or two, Stuart reappears, looking very pleased with himself, clutching an old tobacco tin. He opens the lid and, lo and behold, there's a cardboard box of Swan Vesta matches.

"I once saw Dad burying the box in a secret place at the back of the shelter - he didn't know I was watching," Stuart tells us.

I look at the box of matches, then at Stuart, not knowing how to react. Should I be saying,

"Well done, Stuart," and thinking how lucky we are to have a brother who is so resourceful and can always solve a problem? Or should I be saying,

"This is not a good idea. If Dad hid the tin of matches then it means he doesn't want anyone other than himself using them."

Perhaps I'm worrying unnecessarily. We are used to boxes of matches sitting on the mantelpiece or rattling around in the kitchen drawer back home. We all know how to strike a match to light a fire in the grate. I don't remember Mum or Dad ever saying, "Don't play with matches." Yet somehow I feel uneasy. I stand dithering and worrying about the rights and wrongs of the situation but say nothing. Stuart doesn't appear to think there's a problem.

"Right, lets go. Follow me," he says and leads us to a large clump of gorse bushes alongside the track that the tractor follows in autumn when it's bringing the peat home. He takes a match from the box, strikes it and holds it under a prickly branch. Whoosh! Up go the flames with a sizzle and a crackle and soon the gorse bush is ablaze. Marilyn claps her hands with excitement and sits down on the heather to take off her socks and shoes. Kathleen and I join her and soon we're standing in a row, arms stretched out, holding our socks to the fire, watching the steam rising. Stuart is beaming at us, looking very pleased with himself. He turns and lopes off to take the box of matches back to their hidey-hole in the peat bank.

We stand together chatting and laughing, enjoying the warmth of the fire, listening to the hisses and crackles, watching the sparks dance up into the sky.

Suddenly, we hear a shout from Sandy,

"Help! I think the fire's spreading."

We look at him in alarm. Sure enough, the flames are jumping from one bush to the next until in a flash the whole clump is ablaze, with smoke and sparks billowing into the air.

Stuart comes galloping over the heather.

"Good lord! We've set the Moss on fire!" he announces.

I look at him, aghast. Setting the Moss on fire is a catastrophe.

"What if someone sees it from the main road?" I say. "They'll send for the Fire Brigade! They'll send for the Police! They'll think we're vandals!"

I start imagining the scene. We'll be marched up to the main road, bundled into the back of the Black Maria, taken to the Police Station in Aberdeen. Mum and Dad will be called. The embarrassment! The shame! The minister's family, pillars of the community, supposed to set a good example, accused of a crime! Our picture will be on the front page of the *Press and Journal*. We'll be in court, up before the judge, charged with arson!

"We were only trying to dry our socks, my Lord," we'll plead as an excuse, hoping for a pardon. He won't believe us. We'll go to jail!

I stand rooted to the spot, eyes fixed on the spreading inferno, head full of dire imaginings.

"Quick, Elizabeth," shouts Stuart. "Fetch some water. Sandy, come with me. We'll get the peat spades," and off he runs.

Panic stricken, I look around. Where do I get water? What do I carry it in?

"We can use our shoes," suggests Kathleen.

Good idea! We drop our wet socks, run to the nearest drainage ditch, fill up our shoes with brown peaty water, run back and throw the water on to the flames. The fire splutters for a minute but soon recovers, billowing clouds of grey smoke into the air. We run back to fetch more water. Stuart and Sandy start battering the flames with the peat spades. Back and fore we run with our shoes full of water, dousing the burning branches. Whack, whack, whack go the lads with their spades, bludgeoning the flames into submission. Slowly, gradually, bush by bush, the flames die down. We pour a last dribble of water onto the embers and watch as the wisps of smoke dwindle and disappear. The fire is out.

We stand for a moment to catch our breath and gather our

thoughts. I remember lying in the heather just a minute ago, with this clump of prickly gorse nearby, bright with golden yellow, sweetly scented blossom, alive with the hum of bees. Now it is a blackened forest of dead branches, reeking of acrid smoke. I feel miserable and full of regret.

"Let's go home," says Stuart.

Quietly, we turn away. Stuart and Sandy take the peat spades back to their home in the shelter under the corner of the bank. Marilyn, Kathleen and I sit down and squeeze our feet into our damp socks and soaking wet shoes. As I tie up my laces I look around. I can hear the sound of traffic on the main road but realise that I can't see the cars and lorries rolling by. While we've been fire-fighting, the *haar* has rolled in from the North Sea, hiding everything in a cloud of cold, damp mist. Perhaps it's a miracle sent to rescue us, to hide us from prying eyes. Perhaps no one driving by spotted the fire and phoned the Fire Brigade. Perhaps we won't be up in court after all. That would be a relief!

We head for home. Stuart and Sandy run on ahead, while the three of us girls plod slowly along the track through the heather, uncomfortable in our damp socks and sodden shoes. We trudge down the Glascairn Road, say goodbye to Kathleen at the gate of Gushetneuk, then Marilyn and I climb the wall into the drying green, cross the courtyard, push open the back door of The Manse and go into the kitchen. Mum is standing at the cooker, watching a pan of milk as it heats. Our little sister, Sandra, dressed in her pyjamas, is sitting at the table, drinking a cup of cocoa. They both look up as we come in. Sandra smiles, jumps down from her chair and runs to give us a hug but Mum frowns at us.

"Bairns! Bairns! Where have you been? It's late. It's nearly dark. I called you in an hour ago," she scolds. "And where's Stuart? Is he with you?"

"Isn't he home?" I reply, puzzled. "We've been up in the Moss. He was running on ahead of us. He should be home by now."

"No, he's not come home. What a nuisance that boy is. Where on earth is he? I bet he's gone into the Milne's with Sandy. Elizabeth, go and find him. Tell him to come home at once!"

There's no arguing with Mum when she's cross and so I turn and march out the back door, banging it shut behind me. I stomp up the road and knock on the door of Gushetneuk. Kathleen answers.

"Is Stuart with you?" I ask.

"No," says Kathleen, surprised. "Isn't he home with you? Sandy's home."

"No, he's not come home. Mum's told me to go and find him."

"I'll come with you," says Kathleen.

She pushes her feet into her shoes, closes the door behind her and together we walk up the Manse Road, turning into Glascairn Road, heading back up to the Moss. By this time it's almost dark and the fog is so thick we can't see more than a few feet ahead.

"Stuart, Stuart," we shout but no one answers. Where is he? Is he still up in the Moss. Has he fallen and broken his leg? Is he lying somewhere, all alone in the cold and damp, crying in pain? Has he fallen into one of the old peat banks? Where is he? Why is he not answering?

Suddenly, out of the still night, I hear a low rumbling sound, like distant thunder, coming from over the fence at the side of the road, and feel a blast of hot air on the back of my neck. My heart leaps and I clutch hold of Kathleen in fright.

"What's that?" I whisper.

Then out of the darkness and the mist looms a great grey shadowy figure, lurching against the fence, setting the barbed wires screeching.

"It's a ghost!" screams Kathleen, "It's a ghost!" and we turn and run, helter-skelter, back down the road, as fast as our legs will carry us, desperate to reach the lights of home. Kathleen dives in through her garden gate and I run on, hurtling over the wall and across the courtyard, flinging open the back door, bursting into the kitchen.

"There's a ghost after me," I shriek. "I saw a ghost."

Mum looks at me in astonishment.

"Don't be silly, Elizabeth," she says. "There's no such thing as ghosts. Calm down! You're frightening your sisters. Now, where were you? What did you see?"

I blurt out my story and Mum listens and then laughs.

"You silly billy," she says. "There's cows in that field. You heard a cow snuffling around among the grass near the fence, and maybe hitting the wire with its horns."

"I don't care. I'm not going out there again," I declare. "I don't care if Stuart's lost. I'm not going looking for him any more."

Just at that moment, we hear the back door open and in saunters Stuart, cool as a cucumber.

"Stuart Dunn, what time of night is this to come home?" rages Mum. "Where have you been? I've been worried sick about you."

Stuart sits down on a chair by the door and kicks off his shoes. He smiles at her, his face a picture of innocence.

"I've been up at Glascairn, watching TV with Mr Harper," he answers as if amazed that Mum wouldn't know where he'd gone, and that he was perfectly safe. "He saw me and Sandy coming along the Moss road and asked if we'd like to come in and see his new TV. Sandy said he'd better get on home but I've never seen television and Mr Harper said there was a programme on about motor racing. We watched the Formula One Championships at Silverstone. Fangio was in the Alfa Romeo beating all the Ferraris. It was really exciting. Mrs Harper gave me tea and biscuits. Do you think Dad will get us a TV some day?"

And that was that. Mum chunters for a bit but is soon smiling and asking him how television works, all the while dishing out cocoa to her prodigal son. She's never cross for long with Stuart.

Later on, I'm lying in bed, thinking about what happened this evening and come to a decision. I look back on all the times I've scraped my knees falling off my bike, trying to keep up with Stuart. I remember how many times I've fallen in the sea or the burn trying to leap across rocks like he does. Tonight we set fire to the Moss and, while I'm panic stricken, imagining us being arrested and marched off to the Police Station, thinking it's a catastrophe, Stuart's seen it as a bit of a scrape, forgotten as soon as he's offered tea and biscuits and the chance to watch motor racing on TV.

My brother glides calmly through life like a graceful swan, swimming serenely out of choppy waters, supremely confident in his ability to charm his way out of trouble. I'm more of a tufted duck, paddling furiously in his wake, trying to keep up, eyes darting this way and that, always alert to danger. Nothing bothers Stuart, whereas everything bothers me. He can stay calm and clear-headed in a crisis whereas I seem to have the kind of brain where thoughts rattle around at random, and an imagination that can fly off in all directions. We may be brother and sister but we are very different. It's time I stopped playing *Follow my Leader* with Stuart and made my own way in life.

September

Harvest Thanksgiving

We're walking down the Manse Road on our way to Portlethen Church to help decorate it for the Harvest Thanksgiving Service tomorrow. It's a bright, sunny day with just a few clouds scudding across the sky, but there's a chilly breeze blowing down from the hills in the west, rustling through the leaves on the trees and bushes in the Manse Wood. It's September and all around are signs that autumn is on its way. The sycamore and beech trees that shelter the road are turning brown and orange and yellow, and every now and again a gust of wind sends a flurry of leaves flying into the air, twisting and twirling as they fall down to the ground. I can see clusters of scarlet berries swaying on the branches of the rowan trees on one side of the road, and the plump white snowberry fruits shining like little pearls among the dark leaves of the bushes on the other side. I watch my little sister, Sandra, jump on the berries that have fallen and strayed into our path and listen to the *pop pop* as they explode. I hear in the

Moorland and Meadow: Children Of Portlethen

Rev Alexander Dunn with the elders of Portlethen Church in 1950.
Back row: Mr Still, Mr Walker, Mr Watson, Mr Donaldson, Mr Ritchie, Mr Sim, Mr Wood, Mr Blacklaw
Front row: Mr Adam, Mr Lieper, Mr Crichton, Rev Dunn, Mr Main, Mr Thompson, Mr Milne

distance the twittering of swallows as they perch on the telephone lines and know that, one day soon, we'll come out in the morning to find them gone.

Over the drystane dyke that runs alongside the road comes the sound of a tractor and there's Mr Shand, the farmer from the Mains of Portlethen, busy harvesting, with the binder cutting a swathe through the field of oats, throwing out sheaves on to the newly-mown stubble. Behind come his sons, Sandy and Eddie, picking up the bundles, propping them up two-by-two into stooks. My sister, Marilyn, and I smile at each other because we know that tonight, in the dusk, when the farmer has gone home, we'll be out there with our friends in the field, playing hide-and-seek, burrowing into the tunnel under the sheaves, trying not to wriggle as the straw scratches our legs, or sneeze when the dust and pollen tickle our noses, keeping quiet and still as someone counts,

"Ninety nine, one hundred, coming ready or not."

It might be playtime for us children, but it's harvest time for the farmers, and time for the congregation of Portlethen Church to hold a Thanksgiving Service to bless the crops as they're gathered in. Dad and brother, Stuart, have driven up to the church ahead of us with the boot and back seat full of branches of beech leaves, cut from trees in the Elsick Estate on the hillside beyond Tawse's Smiddy. We are following on foot. Mum is carrying a basket of newly laid eggs from the Manse hens and keeping an eye on little Sandra who is holding onto a small box of dark red gooseberries. Marilyn is cradling two jars of bramble jelly in her arms while I'm clutching a bunch of flowers, picked from the garden this morning. We walk along, round the Post Office corner, past the Jubilee Hall, across the bridge over the railway line, past a row of tractors and trailers parked on the grass verge at the foot of the church brae, and up the gravel path to the door of Portlethen Church. We make our

Stooks of corn in the field at harvest time.

way through the hallway, past the vestry and pull open the glass door into the church.

Sunlight is streaming in through the stained glass window, filling the church with colour and light, but what I notice that is different from usual is the smell of the countryside and woodlands and gardens full of fruit and flowers.

I can see Dad holding a ladder for Stuart as he reaches up to lay a branch of beech leaves along a window ledge, and catch sight of a row of sheaves tied to the railing in front of the choir stalls with ears of corn dancing like little ballerinas in the breeze. There are sacks of potatoes propped up against the communion table and I watch Mr Mann, the farmer from Whitebruntland, and Mr Ritchie from the Mains of Findon dumping down more sacks. Mr Anderson, who farms Barclayhill, is marching up the aisle with a sack of turnips slung over his shoulder. We follow Mum as she makes her way through the church between the rows of pews and carefully sets her basket of eggs on top of one of the sacks of potatoes. Sandra lays her box of gooseberries down on the carpet next to Marilyn's jars of bramble jelly.

I hear footsteps and into the church come the Milne family from Gushetneuk. Mr Milne is a very good gardener, just like Dad, and I can see our friends, Kathleen and Sandy Milne, are carrying lettuce and cabbages and onions grown in their garden. Other people arrive from Findon and the Downies and Portlethen Village, bringing boxes of carrots and cauliflower, baskets of apples and plums, jars of pickled beetroot and strawberry jam, bunches of marigolds and nasturtiums.

I make my way to the vestry and search the corner cupboard for the large brass flower vase that usually sits on the communion table. I find a jug and go outside to the water butt that catches the rainwater from the church roof. I fill the jug, carry it carefully back into the vestry and pour the water into the vase. I start arranging my flowers, pleased that I'd picked them with long stalks so that they would stand up straight in the tall vase. There are purple and mauve dahlias with bright yellow eyes, gold and bronze chrysanthemums with round curly petals, and ruby red and amber spikes of gladioli. When I have finished, I stand back to admire my work and see all the colours of a jewellery box reflected in the shiny brass of the vase. I go in search of Mr Gray, the beadle, and ask him to carry the heavy container up to the communion table for me.

I join Mum and Dad and lots of other people standing admiring all the produce, so many jars and tins, so much fruit and vegetables, so many flowers. I know that Dad is appreciating the kindness and generosity of the members of Portlethen Church. Tomorrow, after the Church Service, everything will be packed into boxes and bags, and then members of the Women's Guild will take parcels round to all the old folk in the parish, while the Elders will load the sacks of potatoes into their cars and take them to the boys' hostel in Aberdeen or to the Church of Scotland Eventide Home in Balmedie.

I glance up at the board that tells us the hymns we will be singing tomorrow at the Thanksgiving Service. It lists just their numbers and so I can't really tell what they are, but I'm sure it will include the traditional Harvest hymns from the Church of Scotland hymnbook, *We plough the fields and scatter,* and *Come ye thankful people come.* I like these hymns but what I'm really looking forward to is hearing the congregation singing with gusto the words of the hymns from the old Sankey hymnbook, like *Bringing in the Sheaves,*

Sowing in the morning, sowing seeds of kindness
Sowing in the noontide and the dewy eves;
Waiting for the harvest and the time of reaping
We shall come rejoicing, bringing in the sheaves.

Then there's the hymn with the title *Labour on,* with the words,

In the harvest fields there is work to do
For the grain is ripe and the reapers few
And the Master's voice bids the workers true
Heed the call that He gives today.
Labour on. Labour on. Keep the bright reward in view
For the Master has said He will strength renew
Labour on till the close of day.

At the end of the service, Dad will stand in the pulpit and give thanks to God on behalf of all the farmers and fishermen, all the men, women and children of Portlethen, for the harvest of the fields, the gardens, the hedgerows and the seas that will feed us and nurture us over the coming year.

October

The Dunn family off on holiday

Holiday at Crieff Hydro

Yippee, it's holiday time! This morning we're off to Crieff Hydro for a week. No more school! No more tattie picking! No more washing dishes! The whole house is alive with hustle and bustle, feet clattering up and down stairs, Mum shouting orders, the dog barking with excitement. Dad has been up since dawn, reminding everyone that we've got a long journey ahead of us and that we need to get on the road as soon as possible. He's driving Mum scatty and I hear her scolding him,

"Alec Dunn, will you stop nagging. I've got a hundred and one things to do. I'm going as fast as I can."

Marilyn and I brush our teeth, tuck the toothbrushes into the sponge bag, and pack it into our small brown leather suitcase. We click the lock shut and carry the case downstairs and out to the courtyard where the car is standing, boot wide open. We pass Mum in the kitchen, brushing Sandra's hair and tying it back with a ribbon, giving lots of instructions to Mrs Moir who's going to be

Moorland and Meadow: Children Of Portlethen

Rev Alexander Dunn's cars

October: Holiday At Crieff Hydro

looking after the house while we're away. Mrs Moir is the lady from Cookston Cottages who helps Mum with the cleaning on Monday mornings but she's come especially today to help us get ready. She's gathering up the breakfast dishes, helping to pack a picnic lunch, while listening as Mum tells her where to find food for the dog, the cats, the rabbits, but that she doesn't have to worry about the hens because Mr Milne from Gushetneuk is going to help with feeding them and collecting the eggs.

Dad's now out in the car, sitting in the driver's seat, beeping the horn from time to time to encourage everyone to hurry up. Mum is tutting with annoyance, running around checking that we've got everything, gathering up the picnic basket, saying goodbye to Mrs Moir. Stuart loads the last suitcase into the boot of the car, slams it shut and climbs into the back seat. Sandra is hugging Magnus, our little dog, and telling him how much she will miss him. She runs and jumps into the seat beside Stuart. I climb in beside her. It's a bit of a squeeze because Dad's car is a Singer, and not very big.

Mum comes bustling out of the house, clutching the picnic basket and travel rug.

"Elizabeth, put that down on the floor at your feet. There's no room in the boot," she says then turns and opens the front passenger door, holding out a hand to Marilyn.

"Come along, darling. You can sit on my knee."

Marilyn is such a bad traveller, and gets car sick if she sits in the back seat. So she always goes in the front so that she can watch the road, which seems to help.

Then it's "Bye-bye, Mrs Moir. Bye-bye, house. Bye-bye Portlethen," and off we go, bumping down the Manse Road, round the Post Office corner, past the Jubilee Hall, past the school, along the road to Tawse's Smiddy and out to join the traffic on the main road heading South. The little car, laden with passengers and suitcases, struggles up the hill out of Stonehaven, then bowls along through

Birthplace of JM Barrie in Kirriemuir

the Howe of the Mearns, past Laurencekirk, past Brechin and on towards Kirriemuir. We drive through rolling farmland with fields of stubble left in the ground after the harvest and rich, red earth where the potatoes have been gathered in. We travel south, following the line of the Grampian Mountains over to the West.

We pass the time playing *I Spy*. Sandra stands on the hump in the floor, which Stuart says is the *transmission tunnel,* with one arm round Dad's shoulder, the other round Mum's so that she can see out of the front window.

"I spy with my little eye," she says, "something beginning with C."

"Cars," shouts Stuart. "Cows," says Marilyn. "Clouds," I suggest.

"No, no, no," answers Sandra, shaking her head.

Eventually we give up. "What is it?"

Sandra is smiling, very pleased with herself. "Cat," she says.

" Where? I don't see any cats," I protest.

"Well, there was a cat sitting on a wall back there," says Sandra.

"That's not fair," we argue but Mum laughs.

"Well done, Sandra!"

Sandra is five years old and has just started learning her letters at school and so I expect Mum is praising her for getting the sound of the letter right.

After a while, we reach the little town of Kirriemuir and slow down to wind our way through the narrow streets.

"There's somewhere special we need to look out for," says Dad. "Do you know who was born in Kirriemuir?"

"J.M. Barrie," says Stuart.

" And what did J.M.Barrie write?" asks Dad.

"*Peter Pan*," we chorus. Everybody knows that J.M. Barrie wrote *Peter Pan*.

"Well, we're just coming up to the house where he was born," says Dad. "Look, that one there, with white walls, at the end of the row."

Dad points to an end-of-terrace house with one window downstairs and one upstairs.

"It's not very big," I say, rather disappointed that someone so famous should live in such an ordinary looking house.

"No, it's not," says Dad, "and it was even more cramped for everyone than it looks. Mr Barrie, James' father, was a weaver and the downstairs room was taken up with the loom where he worked every day. He had ten little children and the whole family lived and ate and slept in the two rooms upstairs."

I peer out the car window and wonder to myself how on earth someone born in a little house in Kirriemuir, where ten children and two adults were squashed into two rooms, had the imagination to write a play like *Peter Pan*. In that story the family lived in a grand house in London, with the children sleeping in a nursery in the attic with big windows through which a boy who never grew up came flying in from Neverland to tell them tales of pirates and Red Indians and a crocodile that swallowed a clock.

The Sma' Glen in Perthshire

We leave the town behind us and drive on through fields of raspberry canes, tied into posts and wires, snaking up the hillsides around Blairgowrie. Then it's on, travelling westward through the forests around Dunkeld, crossing the River Tay, following the river through Strath Bran and into the mountains.

"Are you alright, Marilyn?" asks Dad. "The road's a bit twisty but I'll go slowly. Would you like me to wind the window down?"

Marilyn nods. She's gone quiet and is cuddled into Mum's shoulder with her eyes closed. Poor Marilyn. I know what it's like to feel carsick; it's a miserable feeling. You want the car to stop, but you don't want to be a nuisance. You desperately want the journey to end as soon as possible.

"We're nearly there, darling," says Mum. "And we'll be stopping in a few minutes for a picnic."

"We're in the Sma' Glen now," says Dad.

"Why's it called the Sma' Glen?" I ask.

"I don't know for sure," says Dad, "but I presume it's because it's quite small, not like Glen More or Glen Lyon. Do you see that track running alongside the river? That's an old drove road. Long ago, the

Highlanders from the land to the north used to drive their herds of cattle through the Sma' Glen and down to the market in Crieff."

I wind down my window and gaze out at the world passing by, the mountain slopes covered in purple heather with outcrops of dark grey shiny rocks, and here and there a lonely rowan tree struggling to find a foothold among the scree. At times we drive through dark thickets of pine and larch trees, and then on through open moorland, over arched stone bridges, following the river that runs through the glen. At last Dad spots a lay-by and pulls the car in off the road, stops and switches off the engine.

"Right, it's lunch time. Who wants a picnic?"

"Me, me, me," comes a chorus from the back seat. Marilyn is not so sure she wants anything to eat at the moment.

"Stuart, Elizabeth, bring the rug, bring the picnic basket," says Mum. "Let's find a good spot. What about here, on this patch of heather, by the river?"

We spread out the tartan rug, and Mum hands us mugs of hot milky tea poured from a thermos flask and soft baps filled with scrambled egg. We sit quietly, listening to the sound of the water splashing as it tumbles over rocks in the burn. How peaceful it is! No wonder Dad loves it here. He could follow the road through Forfar and Perth when we go to Crieff but he always chooses to go through the Sma' Glen. He is lying back on the rug, propped up on his elbows, smiling to himself. Mum brings a bar of Cadbury's Dairy Milk chocolate out of the basket and gives us each two squares.

"That'll keep you going till tea time," she says.

We finish our lunch, leave Mum and Dad enjoying some peace and quiet, and wander off to explore. We dabble our hands in the peat-brown water in the burn, pick up pine cones from under the trees, gather anything unusual that we find, a bird's feather, a shiny round pebble, a few strands of sheep's wool hanging from a barbed wire fence.

Moorland and Meadow: Children Of Portlethen

Crieff Hydro

Bay window of the Winter Garden overlooking the putting green at Crieff Hydro

We hear a "Cooee" from Mum, calling us back to the car and we run to join her. Mum is gathering up the picnic things, folding the rug, looking around to see we've not left anything behind.

"Leave nothing but your thanks," she says, as she always does when we go anywhere.

Back in the car, we head south and soon we reach Gilmerton. Then it's turn right onto the main Perth road and into the outskirts of Crieff.

"Who's going to be the first to spot The Hydro?" says Dad.

"I see it," shouts Marilyn. "I see the tower with a flag flying."

"Look," says Stuart, "there's a signpost saying *Crieff Hydro.*"

"Well spotted," says Dad, swinging the steering wheel to turn the car into the long, tree-lined driveway, past the putting green, round the side of the tall sandstone building, slowing to a stop outside the glass doors at the entrance. We have arrived at Crieff Hydro.

"Out you go," says Dad. "Stuart, will you get the suitcases out of the boot? I'm going to take the car to the garage. I'll be back in a minute."

We're standing by the door when up comes a porter dressed in a navy waistcoat and trousers.

"Welcome to Crieff Hydro," he says. "Let me take your suitcases, Madam."

Mum smiles and says, "Thank you," as if she was used to having servants lifting and carrying things for her, and calling her *Madam*. She holds Sandra by the hand and marches confidently through the revolving doors and into the hotel.

I feel Marilyn clutching my hand.

"Can I come with you?" she whispers, "I'm frightened I'll get stuck."

We don't have any revolving doors in Portlethen and so I need to work out how they operate. I wait till one partition glides by then jump onto the mat. Marilyn follows close at my heels. It's a bit of a squash but we keep shuffling our feet, aiming to keep ahead of the panel behind. Round we go and pop out in the foyer next to Mum and Sandra. Stuart and Dad join us. We collect the keys to our rooms from the Reception Desk and then follow the porter along the corridor to the lifts. More excitement! We're not used to lifts either and so this is another adventure. The porter pulls open the concertina doors and we all crowd in. He closes the door with a metallic clang, presses a button and suddenly I can feel us moving upwards and see a wall whizzing by. I try not to think about the fact that we're all in a metal box, hanging suspended by some cables over a deep chasm beneath our feet. I breathe a sigh of relief when the lift stops, the door opens and we can get out. I decide that I don't really trust lifts and from now on I will use the stairs.

We follow the porter along the corridor, past lots of doors with numbers on them. We reach Number 130, which is our room. Marilyn and I are sharing. Stuart has his own room and Sandra has a little bed in Mum and Dad's room.

"Now, girls," says Mum, "I want you to unpack and be sure to hang up your dresses in the wardrobe. You need to get the creases out before dinner tonight and I don't know if we can borrow an iron. When you've finished, come along to our room, number 135."

Marilyn and I explore our new home. This is exciting!

"Can I have this bed? I'm going to put my pyjamas under my pillow," says Marilyn. "Look at these towels! There's a big one we can use when we go swimming. Do you think we'll be able to go in the pool today?"

"Do you see we have a washstand?" I say. "We can brush our teeth here in the morning. I'll put our soap bag in this cupboard under the sink."

We finish unpacking, lock our door behind us and run along the corridor to knock on Mum and Dad's room. Sandra opens the door just a chink and says,

"You can't come in. This is my room."

"Sandra, don't be silly," says Mum. "Open that door at once."

We hear Sandra giggling, but she opens the door and runs off to bounce on her bed and dance around the room, full of energy after the long car journey.

I look around Mum and Dad's room. It's a bit bigger than ours and has a double bed.

"Where's Dad?" I ask.

"He's off to the Winter Gardens to see if there's anyone there he knows," answers Mum as she hangs up Dad's suit in the wardrobe.

"Right, that's everything unpacked. Are we all ready? Let's go and find him. Sandra, come and take my hand. You must always walk along the corridors. Don't run! Remember you're not at home now."

We leave the room, lock the door, and walk sedately along a corridor which seems to stretch for miles.

"This place is huge," whispers Sandra. "It's like Buckingham Palace."

We walk down the stairs, footsteps muffled by the thick woollen carpet, and then tap our way across the shiny wooden floor of the ballroom. There are lots of people milling around and we spot Dad, shaking hands with a tall, jolly-faced man with a very shiny, bald head. They're beaming at each other like old friends.

"That's Mr Lithgow," says Mum. "He's the minister from Auchtermuchty."

Dad is moving on to greet another man and his wife, smiling, shaking hands with everyone.

"That's Hugh Douglas," says Mum. "He was at Glasgow University with your Dad. He's minister in Dundee now."

Dad moves on to chat to another couple and another.

"Does Dad know everyone?" asks Marilyn. "Are they all ministers?"

"Not every guest in the Hotel is a minister," answers Mum, "but there are lots of ministers here at this time of the year. Your Dad will know them from Presbytery meetings or he'll have met them at The General Assembly in Edinburgh."

The winter garden at Creif Hydro

"Why do so many ministers come to Crieff Hydro?" asks Stuart.

"It's because of *The Meikle Trust*," says Mum. "Crieff Hydro was built by Dr Meikle and he was a member of the Presbyterian Church of Scotland. He knew ministers worked hard for the people in their parishes but didn't get a big salary, not enough to pay for a holiday in a lovely hotel like Crieff Hydro. So he set up an endowment called *The Meikle Trust* and that helps to pay the cost of the ministers' holidays."

"Well done, Dr Meikle," I think to myself. "That was kind of you."

Just then we hear the squeak of metal wheels and the rattle of crockery and along the corridor from the Dining Room comes a procession of metal trolleys, pulled by ladies dressed in their waitress' uniform, black dress with white, lace-edged apron.

"Oh good!" says Mum. "It's time for afternoon tea. Let's find a table."

We make our way into the Winter Gardens where sunlight is flooding in through the bay windows and glass ceiling. We weave our way through a room full of glass-topped tables and wicker chairs, past tubs of ferns and palm trees with green fronds arching high above us. We find a table and sit down. Dad comes and joins us, chatting to Mum about all the people he's been talking to. We watch the waitresses working their way from table to table, setting out white bone china cups and saucers, laying silver knives on china tea plates. They reach our table, and set down a silver teapot and a jug full of boiling water on a stand next to Mum. Another waitress brings a three-tiered cake stand, with dainty sandwiches in the shape of a triangle on the bottom tier, scones still warm from the oven on the second tier, and lemon and pink coloured iced sponge cakes on the top shelf. It all looks beautiful, almost too good to eat.

Mum pours us each a cup of tea, and tells us to help ourselves. What a treat! Last week we were out in the fields, tattie picking for the local farmers, with cold wet muddy hands clutching tin mugs of lukewarm tea, chomping on baps filled with jam. Today we're dining like lords and ladies with silver teapots and fine bone china and sandwiches with no crusts!

"Can we go swimming now?" asks Sandra, pausing in the middle of licking the icing off her cake.

"Not yet, darling," says Mum. "You have to wait two hours after you've eaten before you can go swimming."

We look at Mum in dismay.

"Two hours!" I protest. "That's ages. Why do we have to wait two hours?"

"To give your food time to digest," says Mum, "otherwise you'll get cramp."

Mum is a nurse and so she knows about these things. Dad looks at our disappointed faces and says,

"What about having a look around and see if there's something you can do for the next hour? That will give your Mum and I a chance to speak to some friends, and then I'll come with you and we'll go swimming."

That sounds more hopeful. One hour to wait is better than two hours.

"I saw a putting green outside my bedroom window," says Stuart. "What about a game of putting?"

"Good idea," says Dad. "You can collect clubs and balls from the porter at the front door."

"Stuart, you have a watch. Be back here in an hour," says Mum, always a bit anxious if her chickens are not under her beady eye.

We run off to the porter's lodge at the front door, borrow clubs and balls, and make our way round the side of the hotel to the grassy lawn beneath the windows of the Winter Gardens. We find a putting green set out in the form of a clock and work out that we need to stand in the centre and take turns at aiming for the hole at 1 o'clock, then 2 o'clock, then 3 o'clock. To begin with we're hopeless, missing by a mile, hitting the ball too hard, bringing it back to start again. After a bit of practise we start to get better and occasionally even manage a hole in one. Sandra is not very good at waiting her turn, whacking the ball from 5 o'clock to 6 o'clock, not going back to the centre, not really following the rules. She's only little and so happy that we haven't the heart to be cross. We finish the game and then Stuart looks at his watch and says we need to get back. We take our clubs back to the porter, say "Thank you" and go to find Mum and Dad in the Winter Gardens.

There they are, sitting round a table, chatting to friends. I can see Dad sprawled in his chair, long legs stretched out under the table, head back laughing at something. He's dressed in his brown tweed trousers and tan-coloured check shirt – no sign of the dark suit he normally wears, no sign of the dog-collar. He looks very different to the quiet, serious minister going about his work in the parish of Portlethen. I realise that back home he's always on duty, only a phone call or a knock-on-the-door away from having to comfort someone in a time of trouble, arranging to visit someone who is ill in hospital or a family suffering bereavement. Here at Crieff he's off-duty, among friends and colleagues. He can relax and enjoy himself.

Everyone at the table stops chatting to greet us as we come to join them, saying how we've grown since last they saw us, and how proud Mum and Dad must be of their beautiful family. Well, I'm not sure the term *beautiful* is altogether true. I know Stuart is good-looking because all the girls at school tell me he is and Marilyn with her fair curly hair and Sandra with her big dark eyes are obviously pretty, but I'm not so sure about myself. When I look in the mirror, I see someone skinny as a rake with ginger hair and a thin face covered in freckles. Perhaps these people are just being polite, but Mum is looking very pleased.

"Can we go swimming now?" asks Sandra. "Is it two hours since I ate my cake? Is it still in my tummy?"

Mum laughs and says,

"You've been very patient, darling. Shall we go, Alec?"

Dad gets to his feet, smiling at everyone at the table.

"Will you excuse us? We promised we would take them swimming. See you later."

We run back to our rooms, fetch our swimsuits and towels and follow the signposts down the stairs to the swimming pool. We push open the door and take a deep breath of the warm damp air, listening as our voices and footsteps echo in the huge vaulted room. The pool is as still as a millpond, full to the brim of peat-coloured water, piped straight from the springs and burns in the hillside above the hotel. We make our way to the changing cubicles along the side of the pool, swish back the striped canvas curtains dangling from chrome rings, change quickly into our swimsuits, tuck our hair up under our bathing caps and walk gingerly over the slippery tiles to

View from the hill above Crieff Hydro

the steps at the shallow end of the pool. We climb down the shiny metal ladder and gasp as the cold water curls round our warm bodies.

Dad is already in, swimming strongly towards the deep end. He turns with an underwater push against the wall and swims back to us.

"Watch and I'll show you how to swim," he says. "Take a few steps back from the side. Right, stretch out your arms, backs of the hands together and push the water back. Kick your feet like a frog. Try one stroke and then hold onto the side. Well done! Now come back a bit further and do two strokes and grab the side. Now try three strokes."

Stuart and Marilyn and I follow his instructions, swim, grab the side, shuffle back a few steps, swim another stroke, practising over and over again, competing against each other. I'm determined that I'm not going to let Stuart and Marilyn learn to swim before me and they're equally determined not to be left behind. In no time at all, we can all manage to swim halfway across the pool, perhaps not very quickly but we can stay afloat. We are very pleased and so is Dad.

In the meantime, Mum is pacing up and down the side of the pool, keeping an anxious eye on her offspring, making sure we are safe. Mum can't swim and she doesn't seem to want to learn. I think she's frightened of deep water. She has told us the story about how her grandfather and two of her uncles were fishing off the coast of Orkney when their boat overturned and they were all drowned. So she doesn't go in the water but she does like to come and watch and make sure her precious children don't come to grief.

She's busy now blowing up some blue and yellow water wings for Sandra, and laughs and shouts encouragement as she watches our little sister kicking and splashing around in the shallow end. For a moment she is distracted, then looks up in time to see Marilyn perched on Dad's back as he swims towards the deep end.

"Alec, come back!" Mum shouts. "What are you doing? That child can't swim. She'll fall off."

But Dad doesn't seem to hear and on he goes, swimming strongly with Marilyn clinging round his neck. He swims to the steps at the deep end and holds Marilyn as she slides off his back, grabs the handrail and climbs out on to the tiled surface. Marilyn is smiling and obviously enjoying her adventure, but Mum is frowning and not at all amused.

Anyway, Mum says it's time for us all to get out before we get cold and so we climb up the metal steps and run to huddle under the showers for a minute or two. We find our changing cubicle, close the curtains, towel ourselves dry and put on our clothes. We wring out our swimsuits then follow Dad along the basement corridor to a room where there are lines of hot pipes running along the wall. We drape our swimsuits over the pipes and watch the steam start to rise.

"By the time we've had our dinner tonight they'll be dry," says

The Drawing Room at Crieff Hydro

Dad. "They'll be ready for swimming tomorrow, that is if you want to go swimming tomorrow."

"Yes, yes," we chorus. "Can we go swimming every day?"

"As long as you all stay in the shallow end," says Mum, "and don't give me any more frights."

"We will," we chorus.

"Right, lets go," says Mum. "Time to get dressed for dinner."

"Haven't we had dinner?" I ask. "Isn't it tea time?"

As we walk along the corridor to our rooms Mum explains.

"At home we have dinner at 12 o'clock and tea at 5 o'clock, but in Crieff Hydro they have afternoon tea at 4 o'clock and dinner at 7 o'clock."

She turns to smile at my little sisters who are hopping along beside her and says,

"Sandra, you will have a special tea in the Nursery with all the other little children. Marilyn, I don't want to leave Sandra on her own. I need you to stay and look after her. Will you do that for me?"

Marilyn is frowning, trying to work out if this is a good thing or a bad thing. She doesn't like the idea that Stuart and I are going somewhere with Mum and Dad and she's being left behind, but Mum is saying she needs her to look after Sandra and she likes to please Mum and do the right thing. I suspect Mum is thinking that Marilyn hardly eats anything when she's away from home and so there's not much point taking her for a big meal in the dining room. Anyway, Marilyn doesn't argue and off we go to our bedrooms to change for dinner.

We open the wardrobe door, bring out our Sunday best dresses and lay them on the bed. My dress is made of taffeta, and has a dark green velvet belt to match the green checked pattern. Marilyn has a sky blue floral dress with a smocked bodice and cap sleeves. We dress in front of the mirror, brush our hair and then run along the corridor to join the rest of the family.

We all walk downstairs and along the corridor to take Marilyn and Sandra to the Nursery. Sandra immediately spies a big grey rocking horse with flowing mane and tail and runs to climb on board. Marilyn is quiet and holds Mum's hand tightly. When she was little, she used to be terribly shy and would hide behind me and not want to talk to anyone she didn't know well. She's a bit more confident now but still finds strange places and people difficult. However, a kind lady in a nurse's uniform comes to talk to Mum and coaxes Marilyn to come with her. I hear Mum saying that she'll be just along the corridor in the dining room, and they must come and fetch her if there's any problem. With a backward glance to make sure all is well, Mum joins us and we go along to the dining room.

At the door a lady meets us and shows us to a table, set with silver cutlery on a white linen tablecloth. There are crystal glasses and a jug of water but no wine glasses because Crieff Hydro doesn't serve alcohol. That's no problem for our family because no one drinks, except Mum who has a small glass of sherry on special occasions.

Pipe organ in the drawing room at Crieff Hydro

We take our seats and along comes a waitress looking very smart in a black dress with a white lace-edged apron and a starched linen cap. She says her name is Margaret and that she will be looking after us this week. Dad gives her one of his special twinkly smiles and says, "Hello, Margaret," and asks her if she lives locally and how long she's been working at the Hydro. Yes, she answers, she lives in Crieff, walks up from the town centre every day, and has worked at Crieff Hydro for ten years. I can see she's thinking this is such a nice, friendly gentleman. Guess who'll be getting extra special attention this week?

Margaret hands each of us a menu. This is a treat! At home Mum decides what we're having for dinner or tea. She buys what she needs from the shop or the vans that come round the door, cooks the meals, serves them and we eat what is put in front of us. Here at Crieff Hydro, we can choose. I study the menu, and then tell Margaret,

"I'll have tomato soup, then steak pie and potatoes, and then ice cream for pudding."

Margaret writes it down on her note pad. She takes orders from Mum, Dad and Stuart and then disappears through a swing door, presumably to tell the cook in the kitchen what we want.

I look around the dining room. It is full of families like ours, sitting round the tables, some chatting, some eating their meal. Along the wall, near the windows are lots of little tables, each with just one person seated at them, mostly beautifully dressed, grey-haired ladies. I ask Dad who they are.

"These are permanent residents; they live in Crieff Hydro all the year, not just on holiday. Some of them will be widows. Perhaps their husbands have died and their families grown up and left Scotland. This way, they don't have to worry about cooking for themselves, or being on their own."

I take a quick glance out of the corner of my eye because I don't want to seem to be staring. Part of me feels sad that they're on their own, but another part is envious that they're living here all the time, that they can choose from a menu what to eat every evening. They could even go swimming every day!

At this point, Margaret returns with our plates of soup and Mum shows Stuart and I how to be polite and sip from the side of the soup-spoon and not put the whole spoon into our mouths like we would at home. When we're finished, Margaret appears like magic and clears the plates away. We sit and wait for the next course to arrive.

Suddenly the glass doors of the dining room swing open and in come a group of people. Something about them draws the attention of everyone in the dining room as they make their way to a long table near the window. The ladies are elegantly dressed, the men in dark suits, but it's not so much how they are dressed that holds the eye as the confident way they walk directly to their table and take their seats.

"That's the Leckies," whispers Dad. "They own this hotel."

Wow, I'm impressed! They must be very rich. Crieff Hydro is huge and it's not just this building with its ballroom and swimming pool. I know there's a farm and a golf course, as well as stables with horses, garages, tennis courts and gardens. They must be the richest people I have ever seen, but then we don't meet very many rich people in Portlethen. There's Dad's cousin, James Mackie, who comes to visit. Mum has told us that he owns a fleet of trawlers in Aberdeen and has a big house and farm near Insch called Dunnideer. Uncle Jimmy may be rich but, when he comes to the Manse and sits in the kitchen laughing and joking with Mum and Dad, he doesn't seem *posh*. You can tell by looking at the Leckies that they are not only rich but also *posh*.

Anyway, in spite of all the distractions, we eat our steak pie, and then, while Stuart and I have ice cream, Mum has lemon meringue pie and Dad has creamed rice pudding.

"That was delicious," says Mum, "but after a week of eating like this I'll need to buy a new dress because I'm not going to fit into this one."

We finish our meal, leave the dining room and follow Mum as she walks briskly along the corridor, anxious to find out if her two youngest children have survived their stay in the Nursery. Sandra comes bouncing up to us full of stories about friends she'd met and games she'd played, while the Nurse in charge tells Mum that Marilyn has eaten her tea and has been helping her look after the babies. Mum thanks all the staff and off we go to join Dad in the ballroom. He's found us a table and chairs and we sit down, looking around us, watching as the other diners gradually make their way to seats round the edge of the shiny wooden dance floor. We watch the band setting up their instruments on the platform at the far end, plonking a few chords on the piano, tuning the strings on the violin, tapping a beat or two on the drums and cymbals, running fingers up and down the keyboard of the piano accordion. I see a lady approach the band and say a few words and recognise her from the group who sat near us in the dining room.

"That's Mrs Leckie," says Dad. "She'll be leading the dancing tonight."

The lady turns, smiles at us and announces enthusiastically,

"Take your partners for the *Gay Gordons*."

Good, I know how to do that. We dance it at school and at church socials. Stuart grabs my hand and hauls me onto the floor. Marilyn and Sandra follow, and Dad holds out his hand for Mum to join him. The band plays a chord then off we go, march forward for four, back for four, twizzle until you start to feel dizzy, then a hop and step round. I can see there are some English people staying at the hotel who don't know how to dance the *Gay Gordons* and bump into us, going the wrong way, but they laugh and say sorry and so we don't really mind.

The next dance is a *Dashing White Sergeant* and we form a set, Dad in the middle between Marilyn and I, Stuart opposite with Mum and Sandra. We set and swing, march forward and back, raise our arms to form an arch, then duck under to dance with different partners. Round and round the dance floor we go, meeting lots of new people, everyone laughing and enjoying themselves.

Afterwards, Mrs Leckie announces that there are now going to be some dances especially for the children and up we get to join hands for the *Grand Old Duke of York* and the *Hokey Kokey*. I can see there are lots of other children staying in the Hotel this week. I wonder if we'll make friends with any of them.

"Right, boys and girls," says Mrs Leckie, "we're going to do a *Conga*. I want you to form a line, wrap your arms round the waist of the person in front of you and follow me. We're going exploring."

Then off we go, wriggling like a caterpillar, dancing along to the sound of the music growing fainter as we leave the Ballroom and wind our way through the Winter Gardens, into the Drawing Room, round the sofas and chairs, out into the Reception area, along the corridor to the Nursery and back into the Ballroom to be greeted by the sound of clapping from the waiting parents and grandparents.

"Did you enjoy that?" asks Mrs Leckie. "Right, all you little children, it's time for you to conga off to bed."

Mum stands up and holds out her hand to Sandra and Marilyn and tells them to say Goodnight to everyone. I know Mum will be back soon because Crieff Hydro has a babysitting service with staff listening to make sure all is quiet in the children's bedrooms. If any of the babies wake and start crying, they come and fetch the parents.

Anyway, now it's time for some serious Scottish Country Dancing.

"Take your partners for the *Cumberland Reel*," announces Mrs Leckie.

Dad holds out his hand to me, but I hesitate, feeling self-conscious and shy.

"Dad, I don't know how to dance the *Cumberland Reel*," I whisper.

He smiles, reassuringly. "Don't worry. Lots of people won't know the dance. Mrs Leckie will tell us what to do."

Stuart gives me a push. It's all right for him. He's sitting this one out. He's not about to make a fool of himself.

Dad and I take our place in the set and listen to the instructions. It's four hands across, dance round and back, down the middle and back to the top, cast off and dance to the bottom of the set, form an arch and let everyone else duck under and dance through. The steps are easy. I know how to *pas-de-bas* and *skip-change* but it's a matter of remembering what comes next. I concentrate hard and manage to get through the dance without too many wrong turns.

"Well done," says Dad, smiling at me as we walk back to the table. Mum has returned after settling Marilyn and Sandra in bed and says,

"You danced that beautifully, Elizabeth."

Stuart says something much less complimentary but I ignore him. I sit down and take a drink from my glass of juice.

"Take your partners for the *Petronella*," calls out Mrs Leckie.

This time Dad asks Mum to be his partner and off they go to join the other couples on the dance floor. I sit watching them, noticing how beautifully they dance together. I know my parents used to go dancing in the days before they got married, before we were born. Mum has told us one story about the time they were in Shetland when they had just started courting. They had arranged to meet at a dance in the village hall at Ollaberry. Mum was wearing her best dress and was looking forward to introducing her handsome new boyfriend. Dad was late in arriving and, when he did eventually walk into the dance hall, his suit was covered in mud and he smelt strongly of engine oil. Apparently his car had broken down and he'd had to get under it at the roadside to coax it back into life. Mum was cross but Dad just laughed, pleased to have arrived in time for some dancing.

Tonight, there is no sign of mud, no smell of engine oil and they both look very happy, enjoying the rhythm and sway of the dance. It is easy to see all the ways in which Mum and Dad are different. Dad is tall and fair-haired; Mum is quite small and dark-haired. Dad is quiet and calm and thoughtful, while Mum is quick and chatty and bossy, but tonight, while I sit watching my parents dance together, I catch a glimpse of what drew them to each other when they were just two young people working in the Shetland Isles, Dad as the parish minister, Mum the district nurse, far away from home, enjoying each other's company, dancing together in Ollaberry Village Hall. Anyway, I'm glad they did get together or there would have been no "us", no "me" and that would have been a disaster!

One dance follows another until, around midnight, it is all over and time for the band to pack up and go home and all of us guests to make our way back to our rooms. As I snuggle down in bed, I think about everything we've done today. We've picnicked by a river, and danced in a ballroom. We've learned to swim and play clock golf. We've been able to choose what to eat from a menu and been served meals by a waitress. There's been so many new and exciting things already, and more to come. Tomorrow we're going to climb right to the top of the hill behind the Hotel, and then Dad says he'll teach us how to play badminton and snooker and table tennis. We're going to go with Sandra to the stables to see the horses and little Shetland ponies and then Mum would like us all to go for a drive along the side of Loch Earn to see the scenery. I'm hoping we'll be able to go swimming every day and that we'll make lots of new friends with the other children staying in the hotel. As I say my prayers, I give thanks that we are here on holiday in Crieff Hydro, and drift off to sleep in this most magical of places.

November

The Manse, Portlethen, with the walled garden, courtyard, barns and stables, the Glebe, the Manse Road and Gushetneuk.

The Flood

It's Saturday morning and I wake up in our bedroom in the Manse to the sound of rain lashing against the glass in the window and gusts of wind rattling the wooden frame. I lie snug and warm under my quilt, listening to the storm raging outside, then climb out of bed and tiptoe across the floor to stand at the window. I can see lots of dark clouds scudding across the sky above Cairnwell and the hills to the west, and the branches of the trees in the Manse Wood swaying in the wind. I watch the rain streaming down the slates on the roof of the barn, overflowing the gutters, cascading onto the gravel in the courtyard below. This morning, there's no sign of the hens out scratching and pecking among the grass and weeds around the courtyard. I expect they're huddled together on their perches in the barn, fluffing up their feathers to keep warm.

Just then I hear my sister, Marilyn, begin to stir in her bed and a sleepy voice whispering,

"Libby, what are you doing?"

"I'm watching the rain," I answer. "It's bucketing down."

Marilyn comes to join me and together we stand looking out at the world as the wind blows and the rain pours down.

"It's just like the story of Noah and the flood in the Bible," I observe. "Remember where it says,

On that day all the fountains of the great deep burst forth and the windows of the heavens were opened."

"It's not going to rain for forty days and forty nights, is it?" asks Marilyn in alarm.

"I hope not," I answer.

We get dressed and go downstairs to join the rest of the family in the kitchen and eat our breakfast.

"So what're we all going to do this morning?" asks Mum.

Dad buries his head in the newspaper. He doesn't need to answer because we all know he disappears into his study on a Saturday to write his sermon. Mum casts her beady eye over the rest of us. Nobody's allowed to be idle in this house, no matter what the weather.

"Stuart, I need you to bring me in some peat and coal," says Mum. She hardly ever asks my brother, Stuart, to do any housework. He never washes the dishes or sets the table or sweeps the carpets or hangs out the washing.

"He's a boy," says Mum by way of explanation, which is very annoying. I hate housework but the only way I can dodge it is by offering to help Dad in the garden. If Mum can look out the kitchen window and see me busy digging or hoeing or weeding in the garden then she leaves me alone. Today it's raining and so, unfortunately, I can't use that as an excuse.

Mum turns her attention to us three girls.

"Well, I'm going to do some baking. Who wants to help me?" she asks.

"Me," shouts my little sister, Sandra, full of enthusiasm.

"I will," says Marilyn. She actually likes baking, and doesn't seem to mind getting arm-ache creaming butter and sugar for shortbread or beating eggs for the sponge cakes. According to Mum, Marilyn's going to make someone a good wife someday, not like me. She says my poor husband is going to die of starvation because I won't know how to cook or bake for him. Anyway, I keep my head down, staring into my cup of tea, but it's no use. I don't escape.

"Elizabeth, I need you to polish the brasses," Mum says. "Start at the front door and do all the door handles."

Yuk! What a boring, mucky job! Still there's no use arguing with Mum and so I might as well grit my teeth and get on with it. I scowl and stomp off to fetch the Brasso and dusters from the cupboard under the stairs. The trouble is there are so many doors in the Manse and each one has two brass doorknobs. I start with the front door, open it and stand for a minute watching the rain falling steadily on the garden, drenching the leaves on the beech hedge, dripping off the spiky branches of the monkey-puzzle tree. I set to work and, for the next hour, I clean and polish furiously, first the handle on one side of the door, then the other, first downstairs in the drawing room and the dining room, then upstairs in the bedrooms, till my hands are black and smelling like a chemist's shop. At last I'm finished. I tiptoe downstairs to wash my hands in the bathroom, then creep back upstairs to hide in my bedroom, prop myself up on my pillows and read my book. Fortunately Mum is busy in the kitchen and forgets about me and so I'm left in peace for the rest of the morning.

After lunch, the rain turns to a light drizzle and we plead with Mum to let us go out to play. We push our arms into our raincoats, pull on our wellington boots and run outside, up through the courtyard, through the back gate and out onto the Manse Road. We find a line of puddles, some long and thin like Loch Ness, some small and round like duck ponds, stretching from Gushetneuk right down the hill to the Post Office. Sandra is running from one to the other, laughing and jumping and splashing in the muddy water.

Marilyn and I stand for a moment watching Stuart. He has found a stick and is using it to carve out channels in the gravel between one puddle and the next, linking them with canals just like in the Great Glen. I wade into one of the uphill puddles and swish the water with the side of my boot, sending a tidal wave running along the canal into the downhill puddle. Marilyn watches what I'm doing then comes to join me. We form a chain, swishing and sweeping the water downhill from one puddle to the next, enjoying ourselves.

Suddenly, I look up and realise that Sandra is nowhere to be seen. Oh dear! I'm in trouble. Mum expects me to look after my little sister when we're away from home and she's not under Mum's watchful eye.

"Sandra, where are you?" I shout.

"I'm here," comes a little voice from the other side of the drystane dyke that runs along the far side of the Manse Road. I go to investigate. I climb up, finding footholds on the rough boulders and peer over the top of the wall. I can see that the entire corner of the field is flooded and, in the middle of the pool of deep water, there's Sandra, water nearly up to the top of her boots, clutching a jam jar.

"What are you doing?" I ask.

Sandra looks up and smiles at me.

"I'm collecting worms for the hens," she answers.

I climb over the wall, jump down into the water, wade over to where my little sister is standing and take a look. Sure enough, there are hundreds of worms swimming for their lives on the surface of the water and Sandra is picking up their wriggly, slimy bodies and dropping them into her jam jar. I'm impressed! Sometimes my little sister really surprises me. I would never have thought of going looking for worms in a flooded field.

"Wow! The hens will love these," I say. "Come and I'll help you feed them."

I coax her back over the wall where I can see her and know she is safe. We make our way through the courtyard and I watch as Sandra picks up the worms in her jar and throws them onto the ground. The hens rush towards us in great excitement, squawking and cackling, pecking frantically as they gobble up the wriggly feast.

"Can we go and get some more?" pleads Sandra, but fortunately, just at that moment, Mum calls us in for tea. In the evening, it starts raining heavily again and we stay indoors, reading and listening to the wireless till it's bedtime. We fall asleep to the sound of raindrops pattering against the windowpane.

Next morning we are wakened by a shriek from downstairs and hear Mum shouting,

"Alec, Alec, come here! Quick! We're flooded!"

Flooded! Marilyn and I are up and out of our beds and down the stairs, tumbling over Stuart in our rush. Dad is following us, dressed in his Sunday clothes, buttoning up his white shirt and tucking it into his black trousers.

"Look! Look at this!" says Mum, pointing at her feet. "I came down the stairs and stepped into water! Alec, we're flooded!"

Sure enough, the hall is inches deep in dark, muddy water. Dad stands on the bottom stair, quietly watching the way the water is flowing.

"It looks like it's coming in under the back door," he says. "Right, I'm going to get changed. Stuart, go and get dressed. I need you."

Marilyn and I look at each other, not quite knowing what to think. This is interesting, rather exciting, but we can see Mum is not happy. She has buried her face in her hands and is looking quite upset. Dad, however, seems to know what to do, so no need to panic.

After a moment or two, Mum gives herself a shake, straightens her shoulders, and swings into action.

"Right! Elizabeth, Marilyn, come with me."

We sit down on the bottom tread of the stairs, roll up the legs of our pyjamas, and then step down into the water, following Mum into the kitchen. She is pulling towels and sheets out of the airing cupboard, rolling them into sausage shapes and wedging them along the foot of the back door to stop the floodwater seeping into the house. She hands us each a sweeping brush.

"I'm going to sweep the water out of the kitchen into the hall. Elizabeth, go and open the front door. I want you and Marilyn to sweep the water out the front door, into the garden."

Marilyn and I set to work. We roll up the square of Turkish red carpet that covers the hall floor, open the front door and throw the sodden bundle out onto the gravel path. Behind us we hear little steps running down the stairs and there's Sandra, eyes like saucers. She stands on the bottom step for a minute watching us then takes a big jump into the water, landing with an almighty splash.

"Sandra, stop it," I shout but my little sister is stomping around, delighted that her favourite puddle has followed her indoors. She stops when Dad and Stuart, dressed in their old clothes, come running down the stairs and out through the front door, disappearing round the side of the house. Mum is busy sweeping the muddy water out of the scullery, out from under the kitchen table and chairs, out into the hallway where Marilyn and I take over and sweep the water past the hallstand with its coats and umbrellas, and out through the front door.

When we've finished we take our sweeping brushes back to the kitchen and find Mum shaking her head in despair at the dirty puddles on the linoleum floor. We grab our raincoats and wellington boots and go to see how Dad and Stuart are getting on. We find them furiously digging a trench across the drying green outside the back door, tunnelling under the garden wall, diverting the river of water that's rushing down through the courtyard away from the back door and out into the field below the Manse. From there the water will find its way down into the Findon Burn as it must have done for thousands of years before stone walls and houses were built across its path.

Dad is standing leaning on his spade, breathing heavily, watching as the stream follows its new course.

"Stuart, I'm going to have to go and get ready for the Church service," he says. "I'm leaving you in charge. Will you manage? Do you know what to do?"

Stuart is nodding. "I'll be fine, Dad."

I can see Dad wants to stay and guard his house but he has a congregation to look after and a service to take. He props his spade up against the wall and turns away. We follow him back through the garden and in through the front door, leaving our boots on the doorstep. Dad goes to change into his dark suit and white dog collar and we wash and get dressed ready to go to Sunday School. We leave Mum behind, frowning and muttering to herself, "What a mess! What a dreadful mess!" as she swishes the mop over the kitchen floor.

The rain is still drizzling down as we walk up to church, huddled together, sheltering under Dad's big black umbrella.

"Dad, what about telling us the story of Noah's flood at Sunday School this morning?" I suggest.

Sandra hops along beside us singing,

"The animals went in two by two, hurrah! hurrah!
The animals went in two by two
The elephant and the kangaroo.
And they all went into the ark
For to get out of the rain."

We join in till we get to *"the great hippopotamus stuck in the door"* and we are all laughing and everything seems much more cheerful.

"Look," says Dad, pointing at the sky. We look up and there we see a glimpse of sunshine through the clouds and the beautiful red and violet and indigo colours of a rainbow arching across the sky.

"The windows of the heavens were closed," says Dad, quoting the words from the Book of Genesis. "Now we just need to send out a dove to find an olive branch, though I'm not sure there's many olive trees in Portlethen, nor many doves."

Like Noah and his family we have survived the flood.

December

Florence Dunn, Sandra, Alexander Dunn, Marilyn, Granny Dunn and Elizabeth at The Manse, Portlethen

Old Ways and New Beginnings

We're sitting at the kitchen table, Stuart and I, in our pyjamas and dressing gown, watching Dad pouring out hot milk from a pan into three cups of cocoa. He's dressed in his best dark grey suit, white shirt and Glasgow University tie, looking very smart. This evening is special because he's taking Mum out to the Christmas Social in the Jubilee Hall in Portlethen. I can't remember the last time they went out together in the evening, just the two of them, leaving us children behind. Our Granny is going to look after us. I can hear Mum's footsteps upstairs and her voice speaking softly as she soothes Sandra off to sleep in her cot and tucks Marilyn up in bed. Stuart and I are older and so we are allowed to stay up a bit longer.

"Elizabeth, will you take a cup of cocoa through to your Granny?" says Dad.

I carry the cup carefully through the hall and push open the drawing room door. Granny is sitting in the armchair near the fire

Florence and Alexander Dunn with Bootie, the daschund, at The Manse, Portlethen in 1940

listening to music on the wireless. She turns her head and smiles as I come in, but I know she doesn't see me because Granny is blind.

"I've brought you a cup of cocoa, Granny," I say, laying the cup down on the fireside table, taking her hand and guiding it towards the handle.

"Be careful, it's a bit hot."

"Thank you, dear," she says. " Are your Mummy and Daddy ready to go out?"

"Dad is, but Mum isn't dressed yet. She's still putting Marilyn and Sandra to bed," I reply.

I stand watching her bowed head, with its grey curls held in place with kirby grips. She's dressed in her tan coloured, pleated wool skirt with a pale pink, silk blouse and a Fairisle cardigan, and wearing pale grey leather shoes on her feet. I wonder how she always manages to look so neat and tidy when she can't see herself in the mirror.

I try to imagine what it must be like being blind. Sometimes, when I have a nightmare, I wake in the middle of the night, shivering with fear, and need to go to Mum. I slide out of bed, feel my way in the dark along the wall till I find the door handle and let myself out into the landing. I stretch my arms out ahead of me and shuffle slowly forwards till I find the door to Mum and Dad's room. Mum is always awake and whispers,

"Have you had a bad dream, darling? Come into bed beside me. We'll lie like spoons," and I cuddle down beside her, feel safe again and go to sleep.

I wonder what it must be like for Granny, always waking in the dark, feeling her way everywhere, frightened of bumping into things or falling down stairs. I feel sad knowing she's not able to watch us playing, not able to go for a walk outside when the sun is shining unless someone is there to hold her hand, not able to read and sew and do all the things she used to do.

Granny Dunn came from her home in Beith to live with us in Portlethen when Stuart was a baby. I never knew Grandpa Dunn; he died when Dad was working in Shetland. Granny Dunn stayed on in her home in Beith, but then she started to go blind and couldn't manage on her own. So when Mum and Dad moved into their new home in Portlethen, they brought Granny to live with them in the Manse. She has the small bedroom off Dad's study with a bed and a desk where she often sits writing letters to friends back in Beith. Sometimes I stand and watch her using a frame with strings of elastic to help her write in a straight line, her left hand following her words so that she doesn't write over the top of what she's already written. She has an armchair at the window so that she can look out over the garden and fields except she doesn't see anything, but she listens to the wireless and, when Dad is in his study, he opens the door so that he can talk to her.

When Granny Dunn first came to live in The Manse, she could still see a little but ever since I can remember, Granny has been completely blind and I've been fetching things for her and leading her around all my life. Tonight, I watch her sipping her cocoa.

"Will you be alright?" I ask.

"I'm fine, dear," says Granny, raising her head to smile at me. I look into her clouded grey eyes and think,

"How can you say that? You're not really fine. You're blind," and yet she sits quietly and patiently in her chair every day. She never seems bored or restless, and never complains.

I leave Granny Dunn in the drawing room and go back to the kitchen. I collect my cup of cocoa and carry it upstairs to Mum and Dad's bedroom. I peep round the door and see Mum, wearing her best navy silk dress, sitting on the stool at the dressing table.

"Can I come in and watch you get ready?" I ask.

"Yes, of course," smiles Mum. I watch in the mirror as she smoothes a little Nivea cream all over her face. Then out of the drawer comes a fluffy pink powder puff and she dabs a touch of powder over her nose and cheeks. She touches her lips with a little pink lipstick, blots it with a handkerchief till only the faintest trace of colour is left. She combs her dark shiny hair and tucks it neatly behind her ears. Next she screws the top off a small purple glass bottle of *Evening in Paris* perfume, takes a tiny amount on her finger and dabs it on her wrists and behind her ears.

"Can I smell?" I ask. She passes the bottle to me and I hold it to my nose and sniff.

"Mm. It smells of flowers," I say.

Mum smiles at me in the mirror.

"Will I do?" she asks.

"You look very pretty," I say, and think how nice it is to see Mum dressed up and looking happy. I know she is excited to be going out to a dance with Dad. When we go on holiday in October to Crieff Hydro, I've watched them dancing together, sometimes a *Quickstep*, sometimes a *Foxtrot*, gliding over the floor together, steps matching perfectly. I know Dad did a lot of dancing when he was a student in Glasgow but I wonder where Mum learned to dance so well? I could understand if it was a *Gay Gordons* or an *Eightsome Reel* because she would have danced these in village halls in Orkney but I wonder where she learned to dance the *Quickstep*? I must ask her sometime, but not now.

"Right, I just need a comb and a clean handkerchief in my handbag and I'm ready. Now where's my coat?"

I follow Mum downstairs to join Dad, and go with Stuart to the front door to see them off. Mum is giving us some last minute instructions.

"Stuart, you know where we are. Come and fetch us if there's an emergency. Or you can phone Gushetneuk. Eileen Milne will be at home looking after Kathleen and Sandy."

"Elizabeth, I've told your Granny you and Stuart can stay up till 9 o'clock but then you must both go to bed. Do you hear me?"

"Yes, Mum," we say.

We watch as she takes Dad's arm and they walk side by side up the gravel path, out through the gate and into the darkness. We make our way back into the drawing room. Stuart throws another peat onto the fire and then lies on the floor playing with his cars and trucks, running them along lines in the carpet pretending they are roads. I sit on the fireside rug at Granny's feet and watch the flames dancing in the fire, listening to the hiss and pop and crackle of the peat as it burns. Granny sits in her chair, sometimes resting quietly with her hands in her lap, sometimes talking gently to me, reaching out a hand to stroke my hair. After some time, the clock on the mantelpiece strikes nine o'clock.

"Is it time for bed?" asks Granny.

Stuart stops what he's doing, lifts his cars into a box. We know we are not allowed to leave toys in the drawing room because this is where people from the congregation come to talk to Dad. I stand up and give Granny a kiss on the cheek.

"Goodnight, Granny," we say as we leave the room, shutting the door behind us.

"Goodnight, dears," she answers.

I follow Stuart upstairs. On the landing, he turns to me and says, "I'm not really sleepy. Do you want to play something?"

I look at him in surprise. Usually, when Mum is in charge, we go upstairs to our bedrooms right away. We can read in bed for a little while but we have to be quiet otherwise we'll hear Mum's feet stomping upstairs and know she's come to read the riot act. But, tonight, Mum is not here and Granny is never cross with us.

I hesitate for a moment but I'm used to following Stuart's lead, going along with his suggestions, wherever they may take me.

"OK. What'll we play?" I ask.

"How about Hide and Seek?" he says. "My bed is *home*. I'll count up to twenty. You go and hide."

He opens his bedroom door and I hear him start counting, "One Two Three."

I tiptoe into the front bedroom, where visitors stay when they come to the Manse, and hide under the bed.

"Nineteen. Twenty," I hear. "Coming ready or not."

I listen as Stuart starts looking for me, in the wardrobe, behind the door. I hear him go into Mum and Dad's bedroom and I crawl out from my hiding place, sprint across the landing. Stuart gives chase but I fling myself on his bed shouting and laughing, "I'm *home*." We sit for a minute catching our breath. Downstairs we hear the drawing room door open and a wavering voice calling from the foot of the stairs,

"Stuart, Elizabeth, go to bed." There's a moment of silence, and then we hear,

"If you don't go to bed at once, I'm going to go and get your parents."

Stuart and I look at each other, astonished, thinking to ourselves, "That's nonsense. Granny can't go and get our parents. She's blind. She can't go anywhere outside without someone leading her."

"Come on. It's my turn to hide," says Stuart.

I hesitate. My conscience is bothering me. I don't like to upset Granny. I don't want to get into trouble with Mum. Stuart, however, doesn't seem to think there's a problem.

"Come on," he says, "You've had a turn to hide. It's my turn now."

I can see his point. I've had my turn and so it's only fair that he has a turn. I lie on the bed, with my hands over my eyes and start counting. I hear Stuart leave the room.

"Coming, ready or not," I shout and start tiptoeing around the other bedrooms looking in all the possible hiding places, in the wardrobes, behind the dressing table, under the bed. Then I hear Stuart dart from behind the curtains, scamper across the landing, jumping on his bed, shouting, "I'm *home*." I run as fast as I can but he gets there first.

Suddenly we hear a noise from downstairs.

"Is that the front door closing?" I ask.

Alarmed, we look at each other. Surely Granny is not trying to go for Mum and Dad like she said? Surely she's not gone outside? I follow Stuart as we run downstairs, open the drawing room door and my heart sinks at the sight of the empty chair. We open the front door and shout,

"Granny. Granny. Where are you?"

There's a full moon and so we can see right along the path as far as the garden gate, but there's no sign of Granny. Surely she can't have gone far. She can't see where she's going. There is nothing to

The Portlethen Manse with the gravel drive,
monkey puzzle and yew trees

hold on to, nothing to guide her. We stand still and listen. Then in the distance we hear a faint voice and rustling of bushes, far away at the top of the garden. We run up the path, cross the lawn past the line of yew trees and there she is, our poor blind Granny, hands outstretched, feeling along the stones in the garden wall, fumbling among the moss and the ivy, stumbling through the bushes, crying despairingly,

"I can't find the gate. Where's the gate? I can't find the gate."

I feel so ashamed. I take hold of one hand and Stuart takes the other.

"Come back home, Granny," we say, "We're sorry. Come back. We'll be good. Sorry, Granny. Sorry," and we lead her by the hands slowly, carefully back down the gravel path and in through the front door. We settle her in her chair, give her a hug, and quietly climb the stairs and go to bed. I lie for ages, unable to sleep, miserable with guilt.

Next morning, at breakfast time, I open the kitchen door nervously, expecting the worst. Little Sandra is in her high chair, and Stuart and Marilyn are sitting at the table eating their porridge. Mum and Dad are talking about the Christmas Social, who was there, who were the best dancers, the tunes played by the band. Mum is saying how she loves the *Pride of Erin Waltz* and Dad is saying that he prefers the modern dances like the *Quickstep*. I sit down in my place at the table, pick up my spoon and start eating my porridge. I breathe a sigh of relief. Mum and Dad are taking it for granted that all was well last night. Our dear, kind, blind Granny has said not a word.

I spend the rest of the day thinking about what happened and worrying about how to make amends. I start by emptying out my purse, counting what's left of the money I earned tattie-picking in October and deciding I have enough to buy Granny something special for her Christmas. Next I sit down with a sheet of paper and a pencil and write a list:

NEW YEAR'S RESOLUTIONS
I will do what Mum tells me without arguing.
I will learn to cook and bake.
I will learn to say "NO" to my brother when he asks me to do something I know I shouldn't do.

In a week or so, this year will end and a new year will start. It is time for me to leave behind my old ways and make a new beginning.

This is my country,
The land that begat me.
These windy spaces
Are surely my own.
And those who here toil
In the sweat of their faces
Are flesh of my flesh,
And bone of my bone.

A verse from the poem,
"Scotland", by Sir Alexander Gray

Postscript

So our childhood in Portlethen passed by, month after month, January through to December, year after year. My brother and sisters and I grew up, left behind our old home in Portlethen and set out into the world to follow our own path. Stuart took his benevolent leadership skills and his calm, good-natured charm from his boyhood, followed in his father's footsteps and became a Church of Scotland minister, first in Dreghorn, then in Motherwell, before retiring to our old holiday town of Crieff. Marilyn, ever the kindest and sweetest of us all, stayed near Aberdeen to support our parents in their old age, and overcame her childhood shyness to become a wonderfully capable and confident teacher of children with learning disabilities. Sandra used her ingenuity and her playfulness to become Headteacher of the St Andrews Nursery School, filling her workplace and home with little children, fun and laughter and lots of furry animals. I followed my curiosity about the world around me and studied Geography at Aberdeen University, but then chose a profession that reflected a lifelong love of reading and books and became a librarian at the University of Nottingham.

All of us went out into the world and found love and romance. We married, had children and then grandchildren and brought with us all the memories of what we'd learned as children into our new families.

We remembered the teaching of our father, Reverend Alexander Dunn, that *"we're all God's children"* and the example he set us of tolerance and respect for everyone, young and old, rich and poor, men and women, professional teachers and doctors, working farmers and nurses, waitresses in a restaurant, travelling fairground

169

Moorland and Meadow: Children Of Portlethen

Advice Bureau, elders of the Church.

Just as we absorbed the teaching of our father, in the same way we were strongly influenced by our mother, Florence Hourston, and the example she set us of how to be a good parent. She brought us up with warmth and kindness and a lot of no-nonsense common sense. She taught us to value honesty, hardwork, unselfishness, good manners and self-discipline. She gave us the freedom to explore and develop our own personalities, taught us how to be stoical when times were tough, and surrounded us with love and a sense of security. She knew there would be trouble ahead and helped give us the strength of character and the resilience to survive. When I look around the young people in our family today, everywhere I see wonderfully loving, caring parenting of the little ones and feel our mother's influence percolating down through the generations.

It was our good fortune to have loving parents but it was also our good luck to be born in Portlethen as it was at that time. This little cluster of houses, with its surrounding fields and meadows, moorland and moss, steep cliffs and rocky shores, was a wonderfully interesting playground for us children to explore. Over the years we have been drawn back, making regular pilgrimages to our old haunts. We have wandered through the heather in the Portlethen Moss searching for our old peat bank, and scrambled over the rocks down at the shore looking for the rock pools where we used to paddle. We have knocked on the door of The Manse, now called "Glebe House," and been welcomed in by Mike and Carol Plowman

December: Old Ways And New Beginnings

who live there now. We have gone along to the Portlethen Gala and met up with some of our old friends, Kathleen Milne who lived up the road from us, Alasdair Grant who was in my class at school, Elsie Main who went to dancing classes with us, Derek Mann whose family farmed Whitebruntland. We've chatted and laughed and reminisced about the "good old days."

When the four of us Dunn children, Stuart, Elizabeth, Marilyn and Sandra get together we talk about old times, retell the family stories and remember our happy childhood. We are children of post-war Britain, children of Alec and Florence Dunn, children of a Church of Scotland Manse, but also children of the little community where we grew up. We are children of Portlethen.

Sandra, Marilyn, Stuart and Elizabeth Dunn
at the Portlethen Gala in 2017